Love Online

by

Martin Slevin

authorHOUSE®

AuthorHouse™
1663 Liberty Drive, Suite 200
Bloomington, IN 47403
www.authorhouse.com
Phone: 1-800-839-8640

AuthorHouse™ UK Ltd.
500 Avebury Boulevard
Central Milton Keynes, MK9 2BE
www.authorhouse.co.uk
Phone: 08001974150

This book is a work of non-fiction. Unless otherwise noted, the author and the publisher make no explicit guarantees as to the accuracy of the information contained in this book and in some cases, names of people and places have been altered to protect their privacy.

First published by AuthorHouse 11/19/2007

ISBN: 978-1-4343-2695-9 (sc)

Printed in the United States of America
Bloomington, Indiana

This book is printed on acid-free paper.

CONTENTS

1. THE PURPOSE OF THIS BOOK

Introduction

At the time of writing there are over fifty million people currently registered on dating sites across the World Wide Web.

With the rise of the internet has come an explosion in information technology, which in turn has made its presence felt in every aspect of our daily lives. We can pretty much do anything on line now; order our groceries, buy houses and cars, book hotels and holidays, and now, even meet the love of our lives! Dating sites have become a huge multi-national business, and there can hardly be anyone left who is not aware these sites exist, even if they have never joined or browsed one.

When dating sites first began to appear around 1995 they were not for the feint hearted. There was a social stigma attached to them, and if you had a date with someone you met on such a site, you would be embarrassed to tell your friends and family where you met them, as the inference was there was something wrong with you, if you couldn't find a date in the "normal" manner. Today that stigma has well and truly disappeared, and a quick check amongst your friends will confirm this. Ask any group from any social class today, and there will be several people present who have belonged to one or more dating sites, and more often than not, will be willing to share their experiences, with you, both good and bad.

Dating sites offer busy people a great opportunity to meet potential partners quickly, cheaply, and easily, in apparent safety. They allow us to chat to people we like the look of before we meet them for real, and they even let us "browse" the market place for what is on offer before we make a few final choices. They're a bit like supermarkets for singles, and it all sounds wonderful. The problem is that not everyone in this world is honest, reliable and trustworthy, and quite often things are not as clear cut as they first appear.

Imagine you have joined a dating site and someone contacts you. How can you tell if the person is genuine? How can you be sure the information about themselves contained in their profile is correct? What if they are simply a con artist using the internet to prey on lonely people who appear to have money, and seem vulnerable to some careful flirting and nice, but insincere compliments? Dating sites contain a cross section of every society, and it naturally follows therefore they also contain the worst and the best elements of those societies. The thieves, con artists, cheaters and scoundrels who fill our courts are also there, and for every dating site happy ending there is a tale of sadness, exploitation and heartache.

The internet is strewn with broken marriages, broken hearts, depleted bank accounts, bankrupts and even suicides. There are real and present dangers associated with dating sites, and it is the purpose of this book to make the potential internet dater, whether they are male or female, forewarned, forearmed, and protected. If you are already a member of a dating site, or are thinking of joining one, then this is the ideal book for you, because in these pages you will learn how to:-

- Spot the serial dater and cheat.
- Discover the real nature of the person you are chatting to
- Present yourself in a way that is both honest and attractive
- Take control of your own profile and be in charge
- Politely but firmly reject people you are not attracted to
- Strike up conversations with people who interest you
- Maintain an internet relationship until you want to take it further
- Catch out people who are not being honest with you

- Gather a circle of new and trustworthy friends around you.
- Have a lot of fun, safely

...............and so much more.

This is the definitive guide to Online Dating, everything you need to know is here. This book will help you develop your own space on a dating site, show you how to create an interesting and honest profile about yourself, attract people of a compatible character, talk to others in a natural but safe way, meet dates in safety, and hopefully build a solid relationship with that very special person, the one you have always dreamed about. As we have said, the bad people are on the dating sites, but so too are the good ones. The genuine, lonely people who are looking for nothing more than someone to love are out there too, and in their millions. It is the purpose of this book to show you how to tell the difference.

TOP TIP:
- Read this book from cover to cover first, then turn the suggestions into action!

Martin's Story

I have always liked intelligent women, and the one I was waiting for was a physics professor at a local university. "Nice legs" I had thought to myself when I had viewed her profile on the dating site. She had dark hair cut into a bob, which perfectly framed a pair of lovely dark, penetrating eyes. We had clicked straight away and began to chat through the site's internal messaging system; and now a week later, I was standing waiting for her at a small country pub, which we had chosen together as the venue for our first date. I admit I was nervous. This was my first date in twelve years.

When I got married I had thought it was for keeps. But then I suppose so did everyone else who has gone through the terrible roller-coaster of a divorce. To cut a long story short, I came out of a twelve year marriage with the prospect of spending the rest of my life alone looming before me. I was so out of the dating scene that I literally had no idea where to begin. I never really liked nightclubs, even when I was the right age for them, and all the other women I knew were either my ex-wife's friends, or people I worked with. My ex-wife's friends were now my ex-friends too, and they were a no-no anyway, and I never fancied the added complications of starting a romantic relationship with a work colleague. All my male friends were now married, and their wives were not too keen for them going out on the town with me any more, I suppose they thought I might lead their husbands astray, as I was the only single male in the group. I didn't want to spend the rest of my life on my own, but I had no real way of meeting women in a friendly, relaxed atmosphere. I didn't want to go out to bars at night on my own, and try to single out some attractive female from her group of friends, that just sounded doomed to failure to me. So where did that leave me? Very much on my own. I am sure this scenario is echoed across the globe by thousands if not millions of men and women alike who come out of long-term relationships, and when the dust settles, wonder what to do next.

I came across my first dating site a few years ago, quite by accident. When I first saw the advertisement pop up on my screen I dismissed it instinctively. I was still a reasonably looking man, not Brad Pitt for sure, but not Quasimodo either. I had a decent job, my own home and car and was pretty much solvent and secure. For the right lady I might still be thought of as a catch, but where the hell was she? A few days later another advertisement popped up, and this time I had a look.

It sounds very naive of me now, looking back, but I remember being amazed that all the people on the dating site seemed quite normal really. It was not at all populated by freaks and weirdo's who couldn't get a date if they were billionaires. They all seemed nice and friendly ordinary people, in fact, they were just like me.

Like all dating sites, then and now, I was encouraged to have a browse. I was asked to enter some personal details about myself, whether I was male or female, the age range of the person, and the sex of the person I was looking for, and roughly how far in miles from my home I wanted the site to search for available matches. I was also asked a few other things like if I wanted to meet a smoker or non-smoker, and a few brief details about hobbies and interests and so on. I was quite vague at the time and after filling in the form, hit the search button. To my absolute amazement about two hundred single women suddenly appeared, who all lived within 3 miles from me, and were roughly the same age. I spent the rest of that evening like a kid in a sweet shop, reading their profiles and looking at their pictures. I selected about half a dozen "possibilities" and then tried to contact one of them through the site's own messaging system. I was told I could look but not touch, so to speak, unless I joined as a member, and so I did.

The experiences that followed formed the basis for this book. I made some mistakes, and had a few narrow escapes, all of which are detailed here, and the hope is that after reading this book there will be no need for you to repeat any of them.

Anyway, so there I was, and suddenly there she was. She had told me she would be in a certain type of car, and she had told me the colour. I recognised it as soon as it pulled in. She parked the car, opened the door and stepped out. She was wearing a well cut black suit, and I remember admiring her legs again as she leaned back into the car. When she finally stood up she had in her arms a huge pile of papers, not wrapped in a binder of any sort, just a loose pile, and she had difficulty locking the car door with this giant stack of papers under her arm. I wondered what the papers were, a strange thing to bring along on a first date with someone.

"Hi" She said, "Sorry if I'm late" She leaned over and offered me a cheek to kiss. "Hope you don't mind but I have a lot of homework to mark for tomorrow, so I thought I could do it at the same time." She bundled past me into the restaurant, spilling papers, and apologising as she went. I picked them up and followed her inside.

I had booked a nice table for two by the window, and the waiter frowned ever so slightly when he saw the bundle under her arm, but he retained his professionalism, picked up a couple of sheets for her, which had escaped from under her arm as she had come through the swing door, and courteously showed us to our table.

The moment she sat down, her left breast began to flash red, and make a whirring noise, like a child's clockwork toy. "Excuse me" She said, plonking down the pile of papers on top of the menu card the waiter had just placed in front of her. She pulled the cell 'phone from the breast pocket of her suit jacket and answered it.

"Can you give us a couple of minutes?" I said to the waiter. He smiled at me politely and left.

"Sorry about that" She said, replacing the 'phone. "So how are you?"

I was about to answer her when the 'phone rang again.

"Just a minute" She said. I began to scan the menu card. The steaks looked good.

My date took a pen from the inside pocket of her jacket, and began to mark the huge pile of papers before her, while she spoke in animated terms on the telephone as well. After about ten minutes of this, I could see the restaurant manager and our waiter standing together by the bar. I leaned over and touched my date on the arm. "We need to order now." I said.

"Order for me!" she replied, and went back to her telephone conversation about something to do with physics, which was completely over my head.

"We'll have the steaks" I said to the waiter, after catching his eye and asking him to come over again.

"One rare and one medium. Mashed potato with the rare steak, please"

I have always liked my steaks rare, but working on the assumption that not every one else does, I ordered a medium one for my date, thinking this would be safe. To tell you the truth, I was beginning to think that if she couldn't even be bothered to order her own dinner, then I was wasting my time with her anyway.

As soon as she heard me say this to the waiter, she started to wave frantically at me with her free hand; her other hand was still holding the telephone firmly to her ear. I didn't know what she was trying to say to me. Finally, in exasperation I stood up from the table, leaned across and pulled the telephone gently away from the side of her head.

"What's the matter?" I asked.

"I'm a vegetarian." She said, and went straight back to her conversation with the mystery caller.

I took a deep breath, counted to ten, and called the waiter back over. He wasn't amused.

"The chef has already started to cook Madam's steak." He replied. "I will see what I can do." With that he flounced off towards the kitchen.

My date continued to talk on the telephone and mark the papers and smile at me innocently. I looked at my watch, we had only been in each other's company for twenty minutes, it seemed a lot longer.

"The chef has agreed to change the order." Said the waiter, "but the manager says you will have to pay for

Madam's steak as well, as we can't serve it to anyone else, I'm sorry."

I was too irritated by then to argue, and simply nodded. The waiter handed me the menu again. I pointed to the first vegetarian meal I came to. The waiter nodded and withdrew for the second time.

I hadn't been on a date for twelve years before this night, but I never remembered them as being like this. I was beginning to feel that I was paying too high a price for a professor with nice legs.

My date continued to talk on the telephone until the conversation ended a few minutes later.

"Sorry about that." She said again. "What did you order for me?"

I shrugged my shoulders, "something with vegetables"

She leaned across the table, "I am an awful nuisance, aren't I?" She smiled.

I suppose I am old fashioned really, but I believe that if you agree to have a date with someone, especially a *first* date, then you set the time aside for them. You give them your time exclusively for as long as the date lasts, anything else is just rude to my way of thinking.

I was past caring, or trying to impress. "Yep!" I answered.

Her face changed. She became suddenly serious. The telephone rang again in her breast pocket and she answered it.

The meals arrived. The waiter placed my steak in front of me. Then he placed "Madam's" unwanted steak in the middle of the table, and couldn't find anywhere to place her plate of vegetable something down, as she was still marking her papers. When she saw his dilemma, she lifted the papers from the table and placed them on the floor by the side of her chair. He put her plate down with a thud, and left.

"I told you I had a busy timetable." She said, and began to eat her dinner. The last thing I wanted now was an argument, so I didn't reply at all.

The next five minutes were spent in agonising silence. We both just ate quietly, and to tell you the truth I was actually relieved when her telephone rang again. During this call she took a page up from the pile on the floor beside her, and began to read it. I have heard that women are supposed to better at multi-tasking than men, but this woman was reading a technical paper, holding a telephone conversation, eating her dinner, and shooting strange looks at me, all at the same time.

Then very suddenly it all went horribly wrong.

It was a few seconds before I realised she had stopped talking. I looked up and she was turning the most alarming colour I have ever seen in a human face, before or since. Her eyes were starting to bulge out from their sockets, and she sat there with one hand still clutching the telephone, and her other hand waving around her left ear. Her mouth was hanging open, but no sound at all was escaping. Her face changed from pale pink to bright red, and then to a deep purple, and the veins on the side of the side of her head suddenly began to stick out. I realised then that she was choking. I stood up and moved around the table to where I was standing behind her. With the heel of my hand I gave her such an almighty thump between her shoulder-blades that her mobile 'phone flew out of her hand across the table and landed with a little white explosion in my mashed potato. What ever had been caught in her throat was also ejected, and she gave a strangled gasp. She fought for her breath for a few seconds, and then seemed to compose herself. She jumped to her feet. She grabbed her telephone out of the middle of my dinner and rammed it into the breast pocket of her black suit. In doing this she had left a trail of mashed potato across the lapel. I reached over to brush it away, but was met by such a killer stare that I dropped my hand immediately. The look said, *"Don't you even think of touching me!"*

She began to gather up her papers in what I thought was an unnecessarily vigorous manner. "I'm going home!" She announced.

She marched out of the restaurant dropping papers behind her, in the same way she had entered it. I picked them up, as I followed her out to her car. She snatched the papers from me, got into the car, and drove away.

I remember thinking that my first date in twelve years could have gone a little better, when the waiter appeared at my side. He thrust a piece of paper at me.

"Your bill Sir."

That was my first date from a dating site. You may be surprised to learn that I never had a second date with my professor, nor ever heard from her again. However, the experience did not put me off; otherwise this book would never have come into existence.

During my time on dating sites I have met some really wonderful people, and have made some terrific friends, including the many female contributors to this book, so that a woman's perspective on things is included for the sake of a balanced view. However, all the advice given here, especially the points on personal safety and security apply equally well to both men and women.

It may seem to you, after reading about my disastrous first date, that dating site romances are doomed to failure. I can assure you that nothing is further from the truth. I had some very "normal" dates after that with some very "normal" women, which I enjoyed a great deal and had a wonderful time. I had a "wide search area" in those days, (more of that later), and had some dates hundreds of miles apart, then I met my current partner, who lived three miles away from me! We went out on our first date to an Indian restaurant and got on like a house on fire. It's now almost three years later and we are still very much together, so it can work, and it does work for millions of people across the world. But to help it work properly you will need this guide book.

My advice to you if you are thinking of joining a dating site but are a little scared of the prospect, is do it! I will guide you every step of the way, and if you follow the "Top Tips" and the common sense advice, you will have a wonderful time, I guarantee it!

TOP TIPS:

- Get yourself a good Buddy as soon as you can!
- Don't assume every date will be the "One" Be prepared to be disappointed a few times first!
- When you do go out on a date, give them your full attention, they deserve nothing less!

Sophie's Story

T he author of this book, Martin, my Buddy, (you
will learn all about Buddies later), has asked me to
tell my story, so the reader will have both a man's and a
woman's perspective on the fascinating world of online
dating. Well, where do I begin? My story starts like
so many other people's with a break-up. What do you
do when you have been in a ten year marriage, quickly
followed by a nine year relationship, then suddenly you
are alone and in your forties? That's right.....panic!

I am not sure whether it was boredom, curiosity
or desperation which lead me down the winding path
of internet dating, but one thing I am now very sure
of, I had absolutely no idea how many twists, turns,
potholes and dead ends the path would put in my way.

Over the months since my break-up, a girlfriend
of mine had been giving me a blow by blow account
of her exploits on various internet dating sites, and
although I had listened with intrigue, internet dating

was for others, definitely not for me. I actually caught myself wondering once how she could lower herself to becoming not much more than a lot in some male auction, how degrading! I admit I was smug, after all I knew without a shadow of a doubt I would never need to attract a man by such means! I was a good catch: no children, single, I owned my own property, two cars, had a terrific job, and was very attractive (even though I say so myself!) for a forty year old. So, easy peasy. Here I am chaps, form an orderly queue!

I waited and waited and actually did very little to find myself a man, then one day I wondered if my friend had been right all along. The proof of this came one night by way of a telephone call from my friend, who had found her soul mate on a dating site, had just spend a glorious week end with him, and they were already talking about picking out furniture! Here I was, eight months after my break up, and not a single male anywhere to be seen. I began to alter my view of dating sites, especially after meeting my friend's new man, he was lovely!

So I swallowed my pride and called my friend. I invited her over for a bottle of wine and a chat, and when she arrived, asked her to help me get started on a dating site. I admit I was nervous. What if someone I actually knew spotted me on the site? But then, what the hell, if they spotted me then they must be there too! Little did I know that within a matter of days my life would change forever!

I paid my money, registered myself, filled in my profile, uploaded a picture and braced myself for a testosterone stampede.

I began by browsing, as everyone does, searching the matches the site will provide you with which it selects from it's database using the criteria you enter as personal preferences. I am tall, so I specified tall men, a certain age range, non-smokers, and so on. Then suddenly there he was! My Knight in Shining Armour at last! He must have seen me too, because amazingly he had sent me a message through the sites internal messaging system! It must be fate!

Well, we chatted for hours and hours my Knight and I, it made me feel like I was a teenager again. Over the next week we talked together every night until the small hours, then suddenly nothing! He just disappeared. I felt desperate, what did I do wrong? Was he OK? Did he have an accident? Sadly no, he was just a "Player". You will learn more about these types and how to spot them later on.

My first encounter with a Player was a painful experience for me. There was no book like this one around then to teach me what to do, and I felt violated. This self-centered man had toyed with my emotions until I was (I am embarrassed to admit it now) quite falling for him, then he simply moved on to fresh meat. I was truly heartbroken, and looking back, very naïve.

I was so stunned that for a couple of weeks I just went through the motions, logging on, hoping to bump into him. Feeling very low, I decided not to bother answering any of my messages, but just to look out for "him". I scanned every message, still nothing from him, day after day. Then one day, out of the blue, I got a very nice message from someone who appeared to be a genuinely nice guy, something told me to answer this one, so I did. I found not my soul mate, but my Buddy, Martin, the author of this book. Little did I know it at the time, but this was to become my mirror image, but in masculine form. I will explain. As we chatted we realised that every experience, every upset, every emotion, heartbreak and problem I had gone through so had he! We began to share experiences, and we laughed together for hours, trying to outdo each other with tales of our experiences on the site. We shared all our stories, our hopes and fears, and suddenly I found someone I felt really understood what I had gone through. I didn't realise it at the time, but getting a Buddy was the single most important thing I had done since joining the site, the reasons why will become more and more obvious as you read the rest of this book. Believe me, everyone attempting to navigate a dating site, needs a Buddy!

So here I was now, armed with my new Buddy, and extremely dangerous! I had my new Buddy and was far more confident than ever before, I had real support. So off I went again, I knew what to do now, I knew how to "play the game" or so I thought! Wrong! What I had not realised was that there were so many combinations of experiences to deal with. Everyone you will chat to is different, and you actually think that you know them, when really you know very little about them at all, only what they tell you. As a great American internet friend of mine once said, "how come everyone on dating sites are either extremely wealthy or have great jobs? Where are all the refuse collectors, check out assistants and bar tenders?"

So how did I wade through the sea of truth and lies? With great difficulty. I have no magic formula, people still surprise me, and I still get caught out! That's why Martin has written this book. If only I had been able to read a guide to internet dating, after all, most everything else in life seems to come with some sort of instruction manual! This book will help anyone, male or female to avoid the pitfalls and dangers, do heed the advice, it is born from the experiences of a lot of people!

TOP TIPS:
- Don't skip any chapters in this book, the one you miss might have the suggestion you're looking for!
- Read it all the way through first before you do anything else!

Dorothy's Story

W hen my husband died I thought my life was over. We had been married for 33 good years. We had our ups and downs like everyone else, but life with Bill had been very good. When he died I think I died a little too. Our children had grown up, got married themselves and moved away to start their own families, and I found myself in my fifties, alone and companionless. I don't really recall my life for the first year after Bill passed away, I think I just went through the motions every day, drifting along with no purpose and no future. About a year after Bill's death, my daughter and I were chatting one day, and she asked me if I would ever consider getting married again. I was quite shocked at the question, the thought of replacing Bill had never even entered my head, nothing could have been further from my mind at the time. My daughter told me about dating sites on the internet, (Bill and I didn't even own a computer), where people of all ages could meet and chat. "It will give you something to do." Said my daughter, "and you might make a new friend or two."

I suppose that was the start of it. My daughter and son-in-law bought me (of all things) a computer system for my birthday, and they set it up for me in the spare bedroom at my house. Very patiently, David, my son-in-law showed me how to use it, and what the internet was all about. I was amazed at the science of it all, and used to spend my days looking at all sorts of things. I thought it was much more interesting than the television.

One evening my daughter persuaded me to join a dating site. I told her I was much too old for that, and anyway, no-one would ever be able to replace her father.

My daughter told me that I didn't have to replace him, I could just make a few new friends, people to talk to, it would give me an interest. So, on that basis I agreed.

I must admit I did meet some very nice gentlemen indeed. They were all very polite and charming to me, and I told them all that all I wanted was a friend or two, nothing more, and they said that was fine. There was one gentleman who spoke to me every day, and as the weeks, and then the months went by, Henry and I became rather close. We talk every single day, you might wonder what we got to talk about, but there were always things to discuss.

Henry lives twenty miles from me, and he comes to see me now every Sunday. We go for long walks in the park together, and sometimes we go shopping. I must admit I would not be without Henry now, and I look forward to his visits. What I once thought was a very silly idea, (these dating sites) have provided me with a new companion, and my life has a direction again. I am very grateful, and I think the internet is a truly wonderful invention.

TOP TIP:

- Realise not everyone is looking for love, some just want companionship, so state in your profile exactly what it is you are looking for!

Phil's Story

I t never occurred to me to take any kind of personal safety measures with women. I had always assumed I would be ok. I am tall and quite muscular, so I suppose I always thought that women were physically weaker than me, and that fact lead me to be unguarded when I met Sue on a dating site.

We clicked straight away, she contacted me one evening, and we chatted for a long time. She said she worked in the next town, about fifty miles from me, and we arranged to meet one evening the following week. I had never heard of the Buddy System then, and didn't think that I needed one, so I didn't tell anyone where I was going, who I was going to meet, or when I might be coming back.

I had arranged to meet Sue in the lobby of a well known hotel about twenty miles from me, Sue suggested it as it seemed to be about half way between us. We would have a couple of drinks in the bar and get to know one another, if it went ok, I suppose we would arrange a second date sometime.

When I got to the hotel I was a little early, so I sat in the bar on a seat where I could watch the people coming in through the main door. Sue had said her picture was a recent one, and so I figured I would recognise her when she arrived.

About ten minutes later this lovely red head walked in. Sue was a blonde in her picture, but when she saw me, she smiled, and gave me a little wave and began to walk over, smiling at me all the time. I just figured she had changed her hair colouring. She looked great, but somehow I knew something was not right.

I bought her a drink and we sat down to talk. The evening went really well, it was a better first date than I had ever been on. Looking back now, I realise it was all a set up. She was very kittenish and playful, and really knew how to turn me on, with the way she used her eyes, and the way she would touch me very lightly on the thigh, or on my leg as we were whispering to each other in the bar. When she suggested we take a room right there in the hotel I couldn't believe my luck. Of course I went straight to the desk and booked a double room with a credit card. I ordered champagne, and we took the bottle up with us.

When we got into the room Sue opened the champagne and poured out two glasses. I remember drinking my glass down, and then nothing. Whatever she put in the glass had a terrible reaction with me.

The maid who came in the next morning couldn't wake me up and called the manager, he couldn't wake me up either and called an ambulance. I am allergic to certain types of medicines, including some types of painkillers, and when they got me to the hospital I was slipping into a coma.

When I eventually came around, two days later I was interviewed by the police. My car, credit cards, and money was gone, and of course so was Sue. During the police investigation it emerged that Sue was not her real name, the picture on her profile was not her, none of the details were correct, and even her email address which the dating site had blindly accepted, had been one she created in a cyber café. There was absolutely no way of tracing her. Apparently she had done this before.

I am still single at the time of writing, but I have not been put off dating sites. However, I use the Buddy Safety System now every single time, because I know that if I had used it with my date with Sue, things might not have turned out like they did.

Martin Says:

This is one of the scariest stories I have ever heard. You may have read "Date Rape" stories in the newspapers, where a man slips a drug into a woman's drink in order to knock her out and have sex with her. This is similar, but the motive was financial and not sexual. Phil is right when he talks about the Buddy Safety System, this is something I will be explaining in detail later on. It pays to remember that there are female criminals out there as well as male, and until you know someone properly it makes sense to be on your guard, and to use a system that has been designed to help keep you safe.

Don't let Phil's story put you off online dating, the chances of something like this happening to you are about a zillion to one, and with the Buddy Safety System in place we can reduce that risk even further.

TOP TIP:
- Use the Buddy System EVERY single time you go on a first date. It is better to be safe than sorry, and your date won't even know the system is in place.

Your Story

S o what's your story? I suppose if you are reading this you must either be a member of a dating site or you are thinking of joining one. In either case, this book is for you.

The previous four stories are all genuine, and are the experiences of four very different people. Everyone is different, and everyone will have their own story to tell as to why they are on the site, but they all have one thing in common, loneliness.

I like Dorothy's story as it shows that it's never too late to start again, and it proves that not everyone on dating sites are actually looking for love, some people are simply seeking companionship and friendship, and that's fine. What ever you are looking for this book will help you to find it. More importantly, it will help you to avoid the pitfalls and the traps that are there to snare the unprepared. Lonely people tend to be quite vulnerable emotionally, and it is a sad fact of life that there are some totally unscrupulous people out there only too ready and willing to take advantage of that.

I would suggest that when you begin your search for Mr or Mrs Right, you begin by outlining in your mind the *type* of person you are looking for. I don't mean a physical type, that's a trap a lot of people fall into. If you specify a physical type, dark hair, dark eyes etc, you will probably get what you have asked for, but unfortunately, you have no idea what that person is like inside. I think it is much better if you specify character traits instead. That is to say, think what your ideal partner would be like mentally and emotionally rather than physically. Think what you would like them to be interested in...if you hate football for instance, then you're asking for trouble if you don't say so in your profile. What happens when the next big game comes along and you want to do something else? During the two years it took me to research this book I cannot tell you the amount of people who have said to me something like,

"He/she was gorgeous to look at, exactly what I wanted, but after I was with him/her for a short while I quickly realised we were not compatible at all, the whole thing was a waste of time."

Time after time, some people seem to go for the same *physical* type of partner, only to be disappointed time after time. I met a man called Steve during my period of research who only went out with red haired women. When I asked him why, he couldn't tell me! I suggested he aimed for a specific character type rather than something as superficial as hair colouring. At the time of writing he's now in a steady relationship with a brunette.

I also spoke with Angela, an American lady who wanted a "soldier" type of man. Again when I asked her to explain to me why, she had difficulty in understanding it herself. She admitted she had entered into a number of disastrous relationships with men she had known nothing about, simply because when she saw them, they fitted her image of her "soldier". This kind of thinking is almost guaranteed to lead to disaster. Assuming you are looking for a permanent relationship with someone, and not just a short term fling, then it makes more sense to seek a partner who is fundamentally on the same emotional and mental wavelength as yourself. They should like and dislike as far as possible the same things as you generally, if for no other reason than it saves arguments, and will always give you both something to look forward to doing together.

TOP TIPS:

- Look for compatible *character* types, not ideal physical types. You will save yourself a lot of heartache in the end, and the partners you will find will be more compatible with you anyway!
- Prepare a list of the things you really like to do, and include them in your profile.

2. HOW DATING SITES WORK

Subscriptions

A lmost all dating sites on the internet these days follow the same format. You can join for nothing to see if you like the site. To do this you will need to fill out a membership form, which usually is very simple and straight forward. You will be asked to provide a username, this could be anything, you don't have to use your own name if you don't want to, and I would advise against that anyway for security reasons. So choose something simple and nice, or slightly funny, people will notice your "handle". A few I have come across which I thought were good included:

Women's Usernames	Men's Usernames
Fireside Fox	*May Contain Nuts*
Soft n Sensual	*Handsome Hero*
Likes Cuddles	*Reformed Pirate!*

For the women I particularly like *"Fireside Fox."* It conjures up a lovely image for me of a very sensual woman lying naked on a fur rug by the light of a flickering fire, (or maybe I should just be back on the tablets). For the men, I think *"May Contain Nuts"* is great. It is humorous without being crass, insulting, crude or rude; and I think women would also find it interesting. So give your username some serious thought. Don't just enter the first thing that comes into your head. This is the name you will be known by, and remembered by on the site.

I would advise against including anything rude or crude, not everyone will see the funny side of that, and it may put potential partners off you. Once you have entered your username, you will need to enter your email address. This allows the site to email you and let you know if another member has sent you a message. It also allows the site to send you a password which you can use to log on, it is a security feature. Some sites will ask you to create your own password, and when entered for the first time the site will automatically email you with confirmation of this. Again this is a security measure. That's generally all there is to it. Once that is done you have a trial membership status, and you can begin to search for partners. However, as a trial member you will be limited as to what you can do on the site. Usually you will be allowed to search their database of members for compatible matches, and if you see someone you might become interested in, you can read their profile. That's about as far as it goes, because if you want to contact them through the site's internal messaging system, or if you want to email them, then you have pay some money and join. Full membership allows you to interact with other members. Some sites have levels of membership, Bronze, Silver and Gold for instance, where each level carries a different membership fee, but affords you greater privileges in terms of having your profile appear higher up the line when you are included in other people's search criteria as an example. Generally fees are not that much, and discounts are often offered for longer memberships. A years membership will often work out cheaper per month than if you just pay monthly as you go along. My advice would be to begin prudently. Just pay per month to begin with, if you decide it really isn't for you, then you've only spent one month's fees and not twelve, which would <u>NOT</u> be refundable should you decide to terminate your own membership early. You could always upgrade later on if you decide you like the way things work.

Also, don't pay for membership to the first site you come across. They are all structured slightly differently, and it would pay you to see ones you like the lay out of before you part with any cash. So join quite a few to begin with, but not as a paying member. Then when you decide which one suits you, which one you feel comfortable browsing on, join at the lowest level. As stated previously, you can always upgrade later on. At the end of this book there is a list of recommended sites you might like to try.

TOP TIPS:

- Join lots of different sites to begin with, but only as a trial member. Then join as a full member the one site you like the best.
- Join on the lowest grade first, you can always upgrade later on.
- Give some serious thought to your username.

Creating Your Profile

I magine you were trying to sell your car online. You would take a few really nice photographs of it, in scenic locations, showing off its best points. Then you would write an in depth description of the vehicle so that potential buyers would get a good idea of what it was they were getting. You would emphasise its many good points, and try to play down its weaknesses a little bit, without giving a completely false impression of what the car was like to drive. You would not want to sell it too cheaply, and you would want the overall impression to be a favourable one. You would want it to look good.

Then why, oh why do people upload out of focus, old photos onto dating sites, say nothing interesting about their lives, and make themselves sound half brain dead when they are creating their own profiles?

The profile is the second thing a potential date will look at, to see if they are interested in getting to know you. The first thing is your photograph. Because your photograph is so important, I have dedicated the next section exclusively to it, but right now, let's discuss how we go about creating an attractive profile.

So what exactly is a dating site profile? In it's broadest sense it is a single page advertisement. It will feature your "handle" or username, which we discussed previously, have a space for one or two photographs, and there will be some general information about you. The city in which you live, your hair and eye colouring, your height, your age, and so on. Then there will be enough space for you to make the whole page come alive with whatever you would like to say about yourself. This is your chance to sell yourself. If this were not a dating site profile but your Curriculum Vitae which you would send out to potential employers, you would be more likely to spend some time and effort on it, to make it sound professional, to make yourself seem worthy and employable. Why should your dating site profile be any different? This is your chance to be noticed, to seem interesting to potential life partners. This is your chance to shine.

Sadly, this is where most people fall down. They say little or nothing of an attractive nature here, and the "browser" quickly loses interest. Try to see it from *their* point of view. Once they have entered their search criteria and hit the enter button, they will be presented with numerous profiles of available matches. People will not read every line of every profile, they simply don't have that much time. So they select a few "favourites" based mainly on the photograph, then they will start to go through the shortlist more carefully, and when it's your turn to browse, you will do exactly the same!

It is at this point, where the browser is actually going to read what you have written about yourself, that will make the difference between those profiles they decide to contact, and those they delete.

Supposing you are a female browser looking for a man. You have short listed say, five profiles you like the look of at first glance. Now you start to go through them one at a time. If the first three have nothing to say that catches your imagination or interest, but the fourth one does, then the first three will probably not be reviewed again! It's that simple. And it works the same way for men browsing women. I actually saw a female profile once where she stated:

"I have no hobbies or interests. I like to paint my nails, sometimes I do them red, and sometimes I do them pink."

I wonder how many men read that, and thought to themselves that she was an interesting person?

Sadly, a lot of male profiles are no better. Many women I have spoken to have told me that they are sick and tired of reading:

"I like to drink beer and play pool with my friends."

Or something equally banal. When you are writing your profile, bear in mind:

IT IS AN ADVERTISEMENT!

Remember the car analogy at the beginning of this section? Okay, so now that we have some idea of what we should not put in there, what *should* we write?

Some time ago I suggested that you should have a mental picture of the character type you wanted to attract as a potential partner. I also suggested that it is much better if you have the same likes and dislikes as far as possible. It therefore makes sense for you to state quite clearly exactly what your favourite things in life are, and the things you really don't care for too much; then you might go on to say how you would spend your ideal day with a compatible partner. Let's try and put some of this into practice, to see how it looks…..

Let's imagine a female is writing her profile. She likes evening cocktails, and the theatre. She likes dining out, and she likes animals, she owns a dog and a cat. She doesn't like motor racing, and she likes to go to the movies once a week. Our heroine might write something like……

"I want a partner who is an animal lover, just like me. Love me, love Rover and Spike. I imagine a partner who would like to go out to dinner, then on to a good play or a movie, where we could hold hands in the dark and discuss the plot and the scenes afterwards. I want a man I can talk to. At weekends we could go into the country for walks or picnics. If you like motor racing please don't contact me, I hate it. I can always suggest something much better to do

with my man on a warm afternoon than watch cars drive around in circles........."

This kind of profile will have one of two reactions on any man reading it. Either he will reject her because he loves motor racing, or he doesn't like pets, or the theatre, or whatever, in which case she would be better off without him anyway, or he will find her interesting, and contact her. If he does like animals, the theatre and dining out, there are several immediate connections right there. So she has <u>used her profile as a filtering system</u> to get rid of incompatible males before they even contact her. As a result, the men who *do* contact her will all have something in common with her right at the start!

Most dating sites try to get new members a few contacts quickly, to give them a "flying start" you might say. The way they do this is to scan the entered preferences of new members particularly, and then scan the database for available matches. So if a new member joins a dating site and their stated preferences find a match with yours, you will be sent an email about them. This is another reason why it is vitally important to state your requirements clearly.

So what about the men? Let's imagine our hero likes football, likes sports of all kinds in fact, likes dining out, and goes jogging every evening for an hour after work. He is into keep fit in a big way, and isn't attracted to overweight women. He doesn't read much, and likes Sci-fi and horror films. He might write something like:

"I like to keep in shape, but I'm not a fanatic. I jog every evening after work, and it would just be great to have a well toned beautiful running partner at my side. We could run through the leafy lanes near my house, then hit the shower together when we got back. After that we could watch a horror movie in bed."

Again there is a <u>filter system</u> going on here. Some women will reject this guy immediately, but he doesn't want those women anyway! On the other hand, some women will love the sound of that profile! So again the ones who do make the effort to contact him will be compatible right from the start. They will probably also jog and be into keep fit and sports, and so on.

So we now know that we need to be honest when declaring our preferences. It is also a good idea to give the browser some idea of scale or intensity to our choices. For instance, supposing you like to go swimming, but only now and again, then state this, as a browser who goes swimming every single night might get the impression you do too, and might expect to go swimming with you six times a week.

TOP TIP:

- State clearly what it is you're looking for! Don't be too specific though, just in general terms. State your likes and dislikes, and describe an ideal scenario with you and your browser doing something interesting together.

Your Photographs

Have you ever heard the phrase, "A picture paints a thousand words?" What does your picture say about you? Does it reflect the inner you? Does it say something about the kind of person you are inside? It should!

I have seen photographs of women on dating sites where they are obviously falling down drunk, dishevelled, and fast asleep. I have seen pictures of men in the same condition, an uploaded snapshot from last year's Spanish holiday, taken by someone who was equally intoxicated. Some advertisement for a future partner!

Most dating sites will allow you to upload more than one picture, if you can, you owe it yourself to do so. Multiple pictures help to show the browser what you are consistently like in your private life, it also confirms that you haven't simply uploaded the one photograph which was taken when you were looking your best.

There is a fine line to be drawn between having a picture of you where you look better than you have in years, because it was taken by a professional photographer with a soft focus lens in perfect lighting, and the type of photograph referred to above where you look like someone's worst nightmare. Try not to make your profile seem too contrived. The danger with showing the great and flattering picture is that when your date finally meets you face-to-face they are disappointed, as you don't look like your picture. The other extreme is where you upload such an unflattering picture that no one asks you out at all!

Something similar happened to me once, where a date I met for the first time looked about twenty years older than her profile picture. She admitted that the picture was actually of her daughter! I explained that she was deceiving anyone who asked her out, and that every date she had was guaranteed to be disappointed, even annoyed, as soon as they realised they had been mislead. She eventually replaced the picture with a recent one of herself. Honesty really is the best policy with all aspects of your profile.

I would recommend you upload three classic pictures to begin with, after that, the other pictures are up to you.

Picture One

The Upper Body Shot

This is the photograph you should use for the main picture on your profile. This is the small thumbnail picture the browsers will see when you are included in their search returns. When they enter your profile this picture will be seen larger than its thumbnail version, and it will be the first of the series of your pictures they will see.

The upper body shot means above the waistline, and it should ideally be taken indoors, in natural light. Seated at a desk or table always looks good.

It is always a great idea to emphasise in a subtle way any good features you think you have on this part of your body. If you think your hair is great, or you have attractive eyes, then let the camera pan in a little closer so that those features are promoted discretely. It is important to be subtle and discrete with your best features, because you're not saying to the browser, "Yes I have great teeth, but that's all there is of me." So promote your best feature by all means, but don't ram it down the browser's throat. If a lady thinks she has a terrific bust, a close up of her bulging cleavage is going to make his eyes pop for sure, but will he be able to take her seriously after that? It would be much better to have the camera pan back a little to include her bust in this shot, she might wear a tight t-shirt, or a low cut blouse, but the rest of the shot remains an upper body classic pose. So her best feature is there to be seen, but it does not dominate the picture. With this one, look very slightly to the side of the camera and smile naturally.

Picture Two

The Full Length Pose

With this one, out of doors is always a nice touch. Leaning on a gate or wall, or standing under a tree nearly always looks great. Try to strike a very natural pose, and arrange it so that the top of your head, and all of your feet are included in the frame. If a woman thinks her best features are her legs, then this is the picture to show them off. She could wear a shorter skirt, and stand upright, smiling straight at the camera from a distance. In this way the feature is included, and he *will* notice it, but it's not overpowering.

Try to always make the way you are in the picture be appropriate to its background. If a man thinks he has a great six-pack for instance, a picture of him shirtless in a library is going to look totally out of place and a little ridiculous, but the same man on a beach, sunbathing at home, or getting out of a swimming pool, would look entirely appropriate.

The full length shot let's the browser see all of you at once, and it makes a good contrast with the previous picture, the upper body shot.

Picture Three

The Hobby Shot

This is where you should be a little more creative. Remember the guy in the previous section who was looking for a jogging partner? This is where he could upload a picture of him running through the leafy lanes near his house. Or the woman we met could upload a picture of her sitting in a restaurant.

Try and make the pictures you present match, enhance, and promote your profile. The idea is for you to present to the browser a *consistent* portrayal of your lifestyle and personality.

If you have said in your profile that you like motorbikes for instance, this is where you should send in a picture of you sitting astride your bike. It emphasises and adds to what you have said about yourself in your profile.

If you happen to like bungee jumping, a picture of you falling through the air with an elastic band tied to your ankle would be very appropriate here!

If you said in your profile you liked reading, then a nice photograph of you sitting in your favourite fireside armchair with a book on your lap would go very well here.

The rest of the pictures you upload are up to you, but whatever pictures you add to your profile try to make them consistent with what you have said about yourself. In this way the profile all fits together and tells the browser a story about the person they are viewing.

TOP TIPS:

- Always upload recent photographs, taken within six months.
- Have 2 classic poses, one upper body and one full length, plus one "hobby" at least.
- Don't have anybody else in the first two pictures.
- Don't wear sunglasses or a hat.
- Don't be sexually provocative.
- Strike a natural pose.
- Have the pictures taken by someone who knows how to use the camera properly, a professional for the upper body shot is a good idea.
- Have the upper body shot as your main profile picture.
- Crop the pictures if necessary before you upload them, and reduce "red eye" if a flash has been used.
- Dress smart, but casual for your pictures, no tuxedo's or ball gowns, they always look totally contrived and unnatural.
- Profiles with pictures get on average 90% more responses than profiles without a picture.

The above points are just guidelines, but if you stick to them you should be ok, and your profile will say something classy about you, which should be what you are aiming for anyway.

Getting Started

Let's briefly review how far we have come already. You have a made a positive decision to change your future by obtaining a life partner through an internet dating site. You have selected several sites and joined them all as a trial member. After browsing the features and layout of each site you have selected the one which suits you best, and you have paid your money and joined it at the lowest level. You have completed your profile, closely following all the guidelines you have been given so far, and you have uploaded a few good photographs of yourself. Now what?

Now you're ready to go! Begin with a narrow geographical search area. That is to say no more than thirty miles from where you live. If you don't have a car, and public transport is an issue you may need to narrow that search area. Conversely, if you live in a very rural area, and houses are sparse, you may need to extend that search area, it all depends on your individual circumstances. For someone living in a city, or a small town, thirty miles is about right.

Consider the age range of potential partners. If you are a male of fifty-five, and you search for eighteen year old female college students, don't be too disappointed if the ones you contact don't readily respond with offers of marriage. Be realistic. From experience five years either side of your own age is a good place to start. So if you are thirty-five for instance, search between thirty and forty, but again this is a very personal issue and I will leave that up to you.

Many sites these days give you the option of entering whether or not you are a smoker. Most smokers prefer partners that also smoke. Most non-smokers prefer other non-smokers, if you have this option enter your preference. If you do not have this option, and it makes a difference to you, say so in your profile.

Enter the sex of the person you are looking for. Most dating sites now have gay and lesbian sections, and all the advice given throughout this book applies in all circumstances to all people. The points on personal safety apply equally well to men and women, regardless of their sexual orientations.

Some sites will ask you if you are a vegetarian, vegan or meat eater and which of those lifestyles you prefer in a partner. Again if it's there as a question answer it honestly, if it isn't there, and it makes a difference to you, say so in your profile. You are likely to be asked a series of questions regarding children. Do you have any? If so, how many, and what are their ages? How do you feel about children? Do you mind if your Matches have children? And so on. Once again, honesty is by far the best policy.

You may also be asked for your annual salary band. Some people feel a little uneasy about entering this information, if you feel that way there is usually a "*prefer not to say*" option which you can select. A word of caution here. Don't be tempted to say you earn a hundred thousand a year if you only earn twenty. If you lie you will attract the wrong sort of people to you, and if you say you earn a huge salary you may be just the sort of victim a con artist is looking for, or a gold digger who is only after rich partners. My advice is, if you earn an "average" salary, then say so. If you earn a large or small salary then select the "*prefer not to say*" option.

There may be a couple of other questions for you to fill in, every site is slightly different, but when you're done, enter the information, and hey presto, there they are! A list of people who are available, single and looking for the right person to come along and say "Hi" These are your "Matches" That is to say, people whose stored information corresponds with what you have said you are looking for. Therefore *theoretically*, each one of them is compatible with you to some degree. I say *theoretically*, because each match being compatible with you depends upon two factors:

1. You have told the truth.
2. They have told the truth.

Let's not be *too* cynical here, and assume for the moment that both you and they have all told the truth! So here you are with a list of people who should be something like the kind of person you envisaged right back at the start. These are potential partners for the rest of your life, so the next step is to examine them all very carefully.

We all have gut instincts. As you go through the profiles which the search engine has produced you will be presented with a small picture of each person, their username, usually their age and where they live. You have to click on a picture to read the rest of the profile. Depending on how many there are in your list, you might not have the time to read each one in detail, so go with your gut instincts and delete the ones you simply don't like the look of. This is a very superficial way to exclude people, but what other way is there? I know it's what's inside that counts, but you have to be at least physically attracted to someone to some degree in the first place, so delete those who don't do anything for you right away. Keep deleting until you have a manageable number, about a dozen is good.

If you don't have time to read each of these short listed profiles in detail right now, there is on every site a way to "save" a person's profile into your own *favourites* list, so you won't have to search for them all again from scratch the next time you come onto the site. We will be dealing with favourites in depth in a another chapter. For now, just know the facility is there to store someone whom you like on gut instincts.

When you have the time to spare, sit down and bring up this favourites list. These are the twelve or so people you really like the look of. Start at the top, and open the first profile...

TOP TIPS:
- Be honest about your preferences
- Begin with a thirty mile search area
- Begin with an age range five years either side of yours
- Delete your Match List down to a manageable number
- Save and then read each Favourite's profile very carefully.
- Later on, contact every person on this list.

Reading Profiles

O nce you open a profile you will be able to access all the information the owner of that profile has submitted about themselves. There should be more than enough information there for you to make a decision as to whether or not you wish to establish communication with them.

Take a good look at every photograph they have included. What kind of person sent those photographs in to the site? What do the pictures tell you about the person portrayed in them? Are they smiling naturally? Do they look composed or contrived? Do you like the way they are dressed? Would you say the picture was a fairly recent one? What kind of impression of themselves are they trying to convey to you, the browser?

Now read what they say about themselves. Do you fit in here somewhere? Could you see yourself with this person long-term? Do they talk a lot about themselves, and little about the type of person they are seeking?

If they do, they may not pay too much attention to the person they are going to be with. In other words, will they pay more attention to what they want, than what they can give to you? Another way to interpret this is: *"Are they generous or selfish with themselves?"* Do they say anything about themselves that you find off putting, derogatory to others, or offensive? Do they say anything that you find to be endearing or attractive? Do they seem to have a hobby or an interest which you like or dislike? We said before you should follow your gut instinct, it's good advice, what does your gut instinct tell you about this person?

What does the profile say about their interests and hobbies, their likes and dislikes? Is there a match there with yours? Here is a question to ask yourself: *"If this person read my profile, would they be attracted to me?"* Because they *will* read your profile just as soon as they know you have read theirs! If you make contact with this person, the first thing they will do before replying is to read your profile, so they know a little bit about the person who contacted them.

If you honestly go through each profile in your saved favourites list this carefully, you will know whether or not to contact them. Of course contacting them doesn't mean they will respond, or even reply, but *not* contacting them guarantees they won't! You have to be a little brave sometimes! You could even go so far as marking or scoring each profile, giving each important character trait a score. Like our contributor, Maddie.

Maddie from trustcupid. said:

"I have a rating system for each new profile I am interested in. I rate them out of 10 for each of five categories: Sense of humour, Looks, Career, Connections, (matching interests), and Distance. I try to score them from what they have said in their profile, and what I read between the lines in there. With this system everyone will score between 5 and 50 points. I only contact those who score better than 40."

So you should move carefully through each of your saved profiles, deleting again the ones that don't quite fit the bill for whatever reason. At the end of the exercise you will be left with a set of profiles of people to whom you are definitely attracted. All that remains now is for you to tell them you're available!

TOP TIPS:
- Try to imagine the character of the person who created the profile you are reading, do you instinctively like that sort of person?
- Do you think you would be compatible with them long-term?
- Does their profile make you feel relaxed or uncomfortable in any way?
- Try using Maddie's system, and rate each one honestly.
- Go with your instincts.

Winking, Whispering and Mailing

When you finally decide you want to make contact with someone on your dating site, there are several ways you can go about it. Each site will have its own terminology for the separate facilities available to its members, but basically, regardless of what they are called, there are three basic methods whereby one member can contact another for the first time. I have called them Winking, Whispering and Mailing. Some sites will use one or more of these names, other sites will have their own names, but the methods of contact remain the same.

Winking at someone is where you let them know you have seen their profile and might be interested in establishing contact with them. You do not need to say anything, in fact you will not be *able* to say anything, you simply press a button, which is usually positioned around their photograph on their profile, which will generally say something like: "*Wink at this person*" Or

"Blow This Person A Kiss" Once you press the button, an email is automatically generated within the site which is sent to the recipient telling them that you winked at them. The information they receive will generally include a small photograph of yourself, and your username, together with a link which they can use to access your own profile. Winking is the easiest and fastest way of letting another member know that you might be interested in them. It is up to them to reply if they want to of course.

Whispering is the site's instant messaging facility. It only works when the other party is online at the same time as you. This is where you can talk to another member in *"real time."* That is to say when you message them they will be able to read what you have written almost instantaneously. The drawback is that a member with an attractive profile will build up a number of favourites which will increase the longer they remain members of the site, and will probably talk to these people every time they log on. Some people will be holding several conversations at the same time, and they may resent you "butting in" uninvited. If they do not know the new whisperer, or they refuse to reply, this can often leave a new member feeling angry or embarrassed. However, whispering is perhaps the most satisfying of the three methods, simply because it is immediate. If they do reply to your whisper, then you can engage them in conversation for as long as you both wish to continue the exchange.

Mailing is simply an internal email system within the dating site itself, whereby members can send and receive short emails or lengthy letters. The emails are sent in your username, and the recipient does not know your outside email address.

In summary then, we can give the upside and downside of each method as follows:-

~Winking~

Upside

Quick and easy. You don't have to compose anything. The other party does not need to be logged on at the time. They will see your wink the next time they are on the site.

Downside

An attractive profile may get dozens of winks, yours might not even be noticed. Some people will not respond to winks from a person they do not know.

~Whispering~

Upside

More personal and direct than winking. It establishes a real time connection. Conversations in this method can be very rewarding.

Downside

The other party must be logged on at the same time as you. They may be having several conversations with favourites at the time you whisper, therefore they may not have the time to reply to you.

~Mailing~

Upside

The most personal of the three methods. It gives you time to compose an attractive message. They can read it properly when they have the time to give it their full attention. The other party does not have to be logged on at the same time as you.

Downside

Requires effort on your part, which may not be repaid.

So those are your three choices. My advice to anyone starting out on a dating site is to experiment with all three methods until you find the one which yields the best results for you. My personal feeling is that a wink to someone you don't know will have almost no impact, as they probably get lots. Whispering to someone you don't know can be annoying for the other person, as you might start an unbidden conversation with them just when they are deeply involved in a conversation with someone else.

My choice is the email, especially when making contact for the first time. You can spend some time composing a nice and friendly letter to them, and they will be much more likely to respond if they think you have taken the time and trouble to write to them a special message. If you do wish to try the other methods then I would suggest a respectful and courteous approach, for instance, when whispering to someone you have not contacted before try something like…

"Hello. Do you have time for a chat right now? I will understand if it's inconvenient at the moment, but if you could suggest another time perhaps? I really like your profile and would love to chat with you for a while."

This is much better than simply butting in with *"Hi my name is……."* without any regard to whether or not they are busy right now.

My advice is to email when establishing contact for the very first time with someone. If you are not much of a letter writer then don't panic. Simply take a look at their profile, and mention a few things which you have in common. That's always a great place to start. Keep the first email short, no more than twenty lines at the most, but definitely more than two! This kind of thing tends to work…

"Hello. I came across your profile a few minutes ago, and just had to sit down and write to you! I really like what you have to say about yourself, and especially about the …………………….That sounds so interesting. I like your pictures too, the one (in the sweater) in particular. You look so relaxed. I will be on the site tomorrow night

around nine, if you're around then perhaps we could have a chat?"

The above is good because it's short, to the point, complimentary and friendly. It's not over-bearing and it's polite. No-one would take offence at it, and most people receiving something like that would be very likely to check out your profile straight away.

As always though, these are only guidelines, and after experimenting you will naturally gravitate towards a style and method that works for you.

TOP TIPS:

- Don't take it personally if someone chooses not to reply, it is their choice.
- Experiment with all three methods
- When whispering for the first time be polite
- When emailing, pick up points in their profile to talk about, you are much more likely to get a response that way.

Setting Your Rules

When you first receive a response from someone you have contacted for the first time, or if they have contacted you, there is a feeling of excitement which can become addictive. Let's face it, we all like to have our egos massaged from time to time, and to think that an attractive person has singled us out is an uplifting experience. That can be a problem for some people without them realising it, it's very easy to get carried away by the rush of it all. So now might be the right time to start setting some ground rules.

Let's imagine you have made contact with someone you think is very attractive. You might exchange emails for a while with them, and then go on to whisper to them in real time. Relationships develop super quickly on dating sites, far faster than they would in the outside world, probably because the environment of the dating site is a little romantic world all by itself; it is more focused on one thing than the real world, that is, personal relationships, and so you may form a romantic connection with real feelings for someone much more quickly than you would, had you met them in the supermarket, for instance. It is here the danger lies. You may have had some whispered conversations with this person over the course of several days or evenings, and there is a tendency to reveal aspects of yourself, your secret desires, hopes and fears to this person that you would not dream of revealing to them in any other circumstances, after only a few brief chats. This is how people come to believe they have met their soul mate so quickly, and then, blinded by the excitement and passion of the new romance, make desperately rash decisions about their future; decisions many people later come to regret. People seem to fall in love about a hundred times faster on a dating site than they will anywhere else, and for some, that's the problem.

No matter what your heart is telling you about this person, try and remember that you have in fact only just met them, you only know what their profile says about them, or what they have whispered, or emailed to you, and they are, despite your rapidly advancing feelings about them, still almost a complete stranger to you!

The ground rules I am going to suggest to you are again only guidelines for your protection and safety. They are there to be modified as you see fit, or to discard completely. However, I do suggest that you have *some* ground rules set in stone at this point. Your rules are there to ground you back into reality, and to remind you that despite your fluttering heart, you have in fact only just encountered this person.

As stated previously, relationships tend to move at a faster pace online. Once you have whispered to someone for a very short while, they will advance the relationship to the next level by declaring feelings for you, or asking you to meet them face to face.

Going on dates and meeting potential partners face to face is why you are on the dating site in the first place after all. However, there is a big jump between sending emails to someone, or whispering to them, and then travelling to meet them in the flesh, so to speak. Advancing to the next level should not be rushed, and at this point I would suggest you ask to speak to them on the telephone. There are a few married people on dating sites pretending to be single, both men and women, and if you ask for their home number it's easy to gauge their reaction. If they seem reluctant to let you call them at home there just might be a reason for that. My advice is always proceed slowly and carefully, one step at a time. First the site's email and messaging facilities, then the telephone, then *perhaps* a meeting.

It is surprising how you will build up an image of a person in your mind when you are not given enough information about them. Because dating profiles only give us scant essentials about people, our imaginations tend to fill in the blanks. The dating site is a very two dimensional medium, all you ever really see is your own computer screen.. By adding their voice to the mix before you meet them, you are giving yourself more of a chance to form a correct impression of them. There will be many clues available to you by the sound, and pitch of their voice. It's also harder to lie on the telephone than it is on an instant messenger service, where you can think before you type, and the other person cannot listen to the changes in vocal tone.

Once you have spoken to them on the telephone a few times, where you have rang them as well as allowing them to ring you, and you are happy with the way the conversations have gone, you could suggest perhaps swapping messenger service addresses which are off the site, and chatting that way with a webcam if one is available. By using the webcam, you can see them in their home environment, if that's not possible, then skip this step and continue to chat to them on the telephone, until you are completely comfortable about the idea of meeting them.

<u>Never</u> allow yourself to be pressurised into a date. If you like them but are not ready to meet them yet, then simply tell them exactly that. One of the best things about dating sites is that you are in absolute control of your own membership, and can specify exactly who you will and will not meet, and when. At the end of the book I have included some phrases you can use to turn people down politely if you can't think of any of your own. Incidentally, here is a great tip while I think of it. If you ever find yourself being pestered by someone

who will not leave you alone, after you have told them you are not interested, get your Buddy to email them! Your Buddy only has to tell them they are pestering you, and their actions are being monitored! It works like a charm they will disappear so fast, you'll never hear from them again.

So let's summarise what we know so far, this is my suggestion for a set of ground rules. Add to it, deduct from it, and fashion it to suit yourself, but do have *some* rules in place...

- Spend as much time chatting on the "whispering" facility as you like, until you feel comfortable about moving this new relationship to the next level.
- Speak to them on the telephone for as many times as you need to, until you are comfortable with moving on to the meeting stage.
- Never allow yourself to be pressurised into moving too fast too soon.
- Only agree to meet them when you are satisfied that you have learned as much about them as you can *without* meeting them, and you are comfortable and happy with everything you have learned about them.
- Once the date is set, discuss all arrangements with your Buddy. Tell your Buddy, who they are, when, where, and at what time you will be meeting your date.

- Arrange vocal signals with your Buddy to signify how you are, and how you feel, and that things are ok.

TOP TIPS:

- Eliminate pests by getting your Buddy to email them!
- Allow relationships to progress naturally through the stages, one at a time. Email, whisper, telephone, then meeting only when you are ready.

3. MAKING THE SITE WORK FOR YOU

Recruiting A Buddy

There have been quite a few references to the "Buddy System" during the course of this book so far. You may have already guessed what a Buddy is and what they are used for, but just in case there is any confusion or misunderstanding, we will dedicate this section exclusively to the Buddy Safety System, and how it works.

So what is a Buddy, in the context of a dating site? A Buddy is a person you have met through your dating site. A person whom you have come to respect and trust, and who will be willing to take a certain responsibility for your future safety. It is essential they are a current member of the same dating site as yourself. They may have initially contacted you, or you might have contacted them, in either case we will assume that contact has already been established, and during the course of your chatting together you have both come to realise and accept two facts.

1. You both like and trust each other as friends
2. Your relationship will not work out romantically

These are the two essential criteria for the recruitment of a solid Buddy. It will often happen that you come across a person you like to chat to, they might have the same sense of humour as you, or there might be a common outside interest, or you have shared common experiences in the past, whatever the connection, there will be a genuine friendship there. However, you will also have realised that as a potential life-time partner, they are not for you.

Once all this has been established the scene is set for the recruitment of a mutual Buddy understanding. When you are next chatting simply ask them if they would be your Buddy, and in exchange of course, you will be theirs. Buddy's work best when the responsibility works both ways, that is to say you become each other's Buddy.

The type of Buddy we have been referring to throughout this book is an Online Buddy. This is someone who is also a member of the same dating site as yourself. This is the ideal person to recruit, but if you have trouble finding a Buddy online, or you have trouble in trusting your welfare to someone whom you have never actually met, then I would suggest you recruit an Offline Buddy. This is a person who is already a trusted pal. You know them in real life, you probably get together with them now and again for a drink or a chat, and you have come to know them, and to trust their judgement. If you recruit them as an Offline Buddy you are asking them to accept exactly the same level of responsibility towards you as they would if you had met them online. Offline Buddy's tend to be of the same sex as you, as they are already friends, not failed prospective partners, like an Online Buddy usually is. As your Buddy, either of the Offline or Online variety, you will still inform them of all details before you go out on a date, and you agree signals with them for when they call you at the start of the date. It is also a good idea to show them the profile of the person you have arranged to meet before you go. Now let's suppose you have recruited either an Online or an Offline Buddy, and they have agreed to that responsibility.

So how does the Buddy System work? Let's suppose two people have already come to this arrangement. We will call them Sally and Pete. They chat together on the site, and share anecdotes of dates they have had, and swap amusing stories between themselves. Sally tells Pete she has a date with someone from the site tomorrow night. She tells Pete where she will be meeting her date, at what time, and most importantly, she gives Pete the username and profile number of the person on the site she is meeting.

Let's suppose Tom is the date. Sally and Tom meet for drinks the next evening at 8.30pm. Pete, Sally's Buddy is aware of this, and calls Sally on her mobile telephone at 8.45pm. Due to pre-arranged signals,

Sally is able to tell Pete a range of information as to her safety, and if all is not going well, Sally can use the call as an excuse to leave. The various scenarios might go something like these:-

Scenario One

Sally has changed her mind, and does not want to continue her date with Tom.

Sally's 'phone rings:

Sally: *Hello.*

Pete: *Hi, your Buddy here, how is it going?*

Sally: (Surprised) *Oh that's terrible, I will be straight home!*

Sally apologises to Tom, explains that something urgent has come up at home and leaves safely.

Scenario Two

Sally has not made up her mind about Tom yet, she wants to give the date a few more minutes.

Sally's 'phone rings:

Sally: *Hello.*

Pete: *Hi, your Buddy here, how is it going?*

Sally: *Oh I see, take her temperature and call me back in ten minutes.*

Sally explains to Tom her daughter/mother/sister/aunt/niece isn't feeling well, she may have to go home, she isn't sure yet...

Sally's 'phone rings again ten minutes later.

Sally: *Hello.*

Pete: *Hi, it's your Buddy here, how is it going?*

Sally (if she's decided she likes Tom and he's ok) *Oh that's great news, thanks for letting me know, I'll speak to you tomorrow.*

Or

Sally (if she's decided she doesn't like Tom and she's cutting the evening short) *Oh that's bad. I'll come home right away.*

Of course Sally might still be undecided about Tom, in which case she would ask for a regular update on the "patient", and Pete would continue to call Sally at regular intervals throughout the evening until either she tells him she's leaving, or she gives him the signal that everything is ok.

Scenario Three

<u>Sally has already made up her mind that Tom's ok, and Pete has nothing to worry about.</u>

Sally's 'phone rings:

Sally: *Hello*

Pete: *Hi, it's your Buddy here, how's it going?*

Sally: *Oh great news, I am pleased! Yes that's fine, I will speak to you tomorrow.*

Easy, simple, and safe!

Before we move on, a word about social etiquette and the use of mobile telephones in public places. Most men will have their telephone either on a belt or in their pocket, so when they sit down, they put the 'phone on the table in front of them. Most women will carry their 'phone in a purse or handbag, and when they sit down, they will place the bag at their feet. The problem here is that you are expecting your Buddy to call you in a few minutes, and you might not hear the telephone ringing, if it is hidden away in a bag on the floor. The best thing to do is to place the telephone on the table when you sit down, and to simply explain to your date that you are expecting a telephone call shortly. Then you can ignore it until it rings. There are some places where the use of mobile telephones is frowned upon, like a cinema for instance. You shouldn't chose to go to the cinema on a first date anyway, as it's not conducive to good conversation. Once you have spoken to your Buddy, it would be acceptable to switch your 'phone off, because you are either happy with your date, in which case you won't need it again, or you are not; in which case you should be leaving anyway.

There is another way to work this which is brutally effective, but it requires you to be blunt, and some people are either a little embarrassed to do it, or don't want to appear to be so direct on a first date. It goes like this.

Sally's 'phone rings:

Sally: *Hello*

Pete: *Hi, it's your Buddy here, how's it going?*

Sally: *I haven't decided yet, call me back in ten minutes!*

Sally to Tom: *That was my Buddy Pete from our dating site, he's just checking up to make sure I am ok. I told him I was meeting you here tonight, and he's checked out your profile. I hope you don't mind. Let's face it you can't be too careful these days, you could be a homicidal maniac for all I know!"* (big smile!).

I know a lady on one of the UK dating sites who used to say exactly that word for word. After the initial surprise her dates were always fine about it. In fact most of them congratulated her on her good solid sense. If Tom is ok, then he won't mind Sally taking precautions for her own safety, and if Tom is *not* ok, then this is the kind of thing that is sure to put him off stepping out of line. He now knows that there is someone out there looking over Sally's shoulder, someone who knows who Tom is! This particular technique is a little too direct for some people, for other's it will be ideal. Whatever your personal feeling I strongly advise you employ one or the other, as the saying goes, it's always better to be safe than sorry.

So, your Buddy checks that you are ok every time you meet someone from the site. Your Buddy doesn't have to live near you, in fact they don't even have to live in the same country, but they do have to be available when you are out on a date with a stranger, whenever that is.

However, a good Buddy will be so much more than simply someone to watch your back. They will offer you emotional support if something goes wrong, a shoulder to cry on, as the saying goes. They will be someone to talk to, someone to laugh about the crazy things that happen to people on dating sites, and they truly will become a great friend. It's worth having a Buddy for that fact alone.

As I stated earlier, all advice given here is intended for the safety and security of men and women. The example of Sally and Pete as mutual Buddy's assumes a heterosexual dating site. If you are on a gay or lesbian site, exactly the same advice applies. You will need a Buddy for the same reasons and for the same benefits, only your Buddy will be of the same sex as you, that's the only difference.

A word before we close. Without sounding sexist, it has often been remarked to me that women need a Buddy more than men. I am told a man would be embarrassed to ask another person to check up and see if he's ok when he's out on a date, my answer to that is read *Phil's Story* at the beginning of this book...

TOP TIPS:

- Make sure your Buddy, whether they are Online or Offline, agrees to, accepts and understands what is required of them.
- Don't be afraid to tell your date you have a Buddy looking over your shoulder. If your date is OK, they will be OK with the arrangement. If your date is not OK, then informing them of your Buddy could be very important!
- Use the system as it is designed. It works, and that is why you should have it..

Mutual Respect

T he more people you to chat to on a dating site, the more you will come to understand that some people behave as though the dating site is an entertainment arena in its own right, and not simply a means to an end. You will discover people, who have been on there for years, have had hundreds of dates and not a relationship in site, ever. Other people chat to everyone in sight and never agree to a date with anyone. Some people will chat with you for a while, and then suddenly and inexplicably never talk to you again, leaving you to wonder if you inadvertently insulted them in some way. It takes all sorts to make a world, and believe me, you will meet them all, for they are all on there. Mercifully, such people are in the vast minority, and dating sites are generally populated with very nice adults who are genuinely looking for the right person to spend the rest of their lives with. I have classified most of the others into types and given them all names, so that spotting them is easier, and they are listed at the back of this book for your own reference purposes.

I have inserted this chapter here, so that you are aware of the fact that some people will try and toy with your emotions, the chances of this happening increases proportionately with the length of time you remain a member, and so that you will have a method of behaving which is dignified and classy, and will not allow you to fall into the trap of lowering your standards to match theirs.

Remember always, that the key to any long-lasting relationship in my opinion is mutual respect. Without respect there isn't much of anything solid to build upon. So when you encounter one or more of these people, who are members of the site because they can't find anything else to do in the evening, you will not be hurt or insulted, nor feel used or abused. You will simply be able to shrug your shoulders and move on.

If you accord to everyone you contact, and to everyone who contacts you, courtesy and respect, then whether or not they do the same, you will be able to hold your head up, and know that you're not responsible for other people's foolishness or immaturity. You will however be able to give your Buddy a good laugh about such people when you call them later.

It is actually a lot easier to be assertive with people online than it is face to face, you just have to get used to it! If someone continually contacts you every time you log on, to the point where you dread seeing their name come up on the screen, and you haven't yet got to the point where you wish to involve your Buddy as discussed earlier, then simply tell them they're crowding you, and need to back up a little, something polite but firm will generally work.

"I'm sorry but I am too busy to chat with you right now. I do have a number of people on here that I plan to spend some time with tonight, and I can't fit you in. Please don't contact me every time I am on here, if I have the time I will contact you next time, ok? Thanks for being in touch."

On every dating site there are also formal complaint procedures you can follow if someone is being a nuisance or a pest, or is becoming insulting, intimidating or threatening. These facilities are there for your benefit, so don't be afraid to use them if all else fails. There is also a *blocking* facility you can use so that the person blocked will not be able to tell when you are present on the site, more about blocking later.

It may appear to you that I am preparing you for a life of harassment and pest control, when in reality nothing is further from the truth. I am certain the vast majority of people you will meet online will be fine in every respect; it's just a fact of life that there are a tiny minority who tend to spoil the fun for everyone else. If you are able to deal with them effectively, they won't come to bother you in the slightest. Just remember not to lose your temper, be offensive or aggressive, as they also have the right to report you! Consistent offenders can be expelled from the site, and not allowed back in. Mutual Respect is the key phrase, even if it's not that mutual at times. Just remain calm and treat them in the same way you would explain to a child why they can't play on the bonfire, eventually they will get the message and leave you alone, and if they don't, you have other resources open to you which we have mentioned earlier.

TOP TIPS:

- Treat every one you talk to with courtesy and respect.
- Be firm but polite when rejecting offers.
- Get to know the "types" and learn to spot them early.

Dating Your Favourites

I f you stay on a dating site long enough you will gather around you a circle of good friends. It is from this circle you will have recruited your current Buddy, if they are of the Online type, as discussed earlier. The other members of the circle will probably comprise the bulk of your favourites list, and you will chat with all or most of them every time you log on to the site. This is an unusual situation for most people to be in. It's not often in the course of our normal lives that a woman would have a group of good-looking men eager to talk to her, and flirt with her whenever she wanted. And of course the same applies for men. This circle of favourites can be very confidence enhancing, as they fall into a strange and unusual category. They are not really partners, as you probably haven't dated any of them yet, and they're definitely not strangers either. Nor are they really friends in the normal sense of the word, as you probably haven't even met them face to face. However, they are "*intimates*" if I can call them that, and they will continue to populate your favourites list and you, theirs, until one or the other of you finds a real partner and exits the site.

The problem with these intimates is that they will take up a large proportion of your time when you are logged on to the site by constantly chatting to you... which means you are not spending as much time as you should be in searching for the person you joined the site to find in the first place, your soul mate. Yet one of these favourites might turn out to be the one you were looking for all the time! So what to do? The answer is to date all your favourites!!!

Let's face it, they already like you, and you like them or they wouldn't be favourites would they? So you may as well go and see them, go out to dinner with them and see how it goes! Don't forget to tell your Buddy the meeting plans though, even if they are your favourites.

One of the nicest things about dating your favourites list is you already know a great deal about them, so the conversation is much more likely to flow very naturally when you meet them, much more than it might if you were on a "cold" date for the first time. You will have already spoken to this person a number of times online before you meet them, so there will be lots to catch up on, the date has a real head-start, and most people will find that some of the most enjoyable evenings they have spent have been with a person from their favourites list. There is a mutual attraction there already, a mutual emotional tie, some shared experiences, a few things in common and a short history, so the chances are the date will go very well indeed. It is much easier to ask out a favourite than it is to ask out a total stranger, there is nowhere near as much pressure as they are already a "friend." Something simple and straightforward would work best here:

"....*We've been chatting for a good while now, and I would really like to meet you, what do you think?*"

The only danger I have ever seen here is that if you decide they are not for you in a romantic sense, after you do meet them, when you tell them that, you may lose them as a friend as well. I am afraid that is a chance you are just going to have to take. Remember this person has a special place with you, as a favourite, so if you are going to let them down, then do it in the most gentle way you can think of. It would be a real shame to lose them as a friend as well, but sometimes that just cannot be helped.

Polly from asiafriendfinder said:

"*I always date my favourites, that's what makes them favourites! But if I decide not to see one of them again, I just say they are a wonderful person, but I can't see us spending the rest of our lives together, but I hope we can stay in contact as friends. That's a gentle way to tell them I'm not going to date them again, and it works. I have never lost one as a friend after saying it this way.*"

Because in a romantic sense, a date with a favourite has a head start, so to speak, on other dates you might go on, there is the danger that you yourself make a commitment with the favourite for which you are not quite ready. Don't get carried away, enjoy the evening and have a wonderful time, but always remember to date the _whole_ of your favourites list at least once, before you decide who you like the best!

TOP TIPS:

- Date the whole of your favourites list at least once.
- Don't be tempted to make a commitment to a favourite too early.
- When eliminating potential partners from your favourites, do it gently.
- Recruit reserve Buddy's from favourites who do not make it as future partners.

Working With Your Buddy

U p until now I have been stressing the advantages you will receive by having a Buddy; I haven't said anything about *your* responsibilities in being *their* Buddy. The Buddy system is designed to offer *mutual* protection, and therefore has to work both ways. You must take an active interest in your Buddy's personal safety, both now and in the future, and take some responsibility towards insuring their future happiness.

There are lots of things you can do to achieve this. You already know to liaise with your Buddy over their arrangements when they agree to a date, you know to call them at a pre-arranged time, and you will have worked out vocal signals so they can tell you without alerting their date how it's all going. But what else can you do? You can take a look at their favourites list for them, and read the profiles of the people they are likely to date soon, you can offer advice on the best way for them to approach each "candidate" and you can suggest that such a person might be a better bet for them than someone else in their favourites. You can even suggest strategies to them if they are having problems with someone on the site, or if they don't know how to handle a particular person. You can just be a good friend. You can also make sure you are very familiar with their own set of *Ground Rules* as described earlier, and when they start to stray, as everyone does sooner or later, you can pull them back on course. If you truly have their best interests at heart, and you should, then the chances are they will listen to you. Get close to your Buddy, and do your best for them. Of course one day their efforts will succeed, and they will find the partner they have been looking for, and when they leave the site you will lose your Buddy, and have to recruit another one from your favourites list, but hey, that's life! When you find what you're looking for they will lose *their* Buddy and have to recruit another one, that's just the way it works.

The type of relationship you will build with your Buddy is an unusual one. It has been known for Buddy's to become extremely close, so close in fact they have been unable to let go of the relationship when one of them meets a partner for real, and tries to resign from the dating site. There can be a feeling of loss, jealously or possessiveness that may surprise you, especially if you have been Buddy's for some time, and have shared a lot of experiences together. The thing to remember is that you can, and probably should remain friends; providing the new partner is OK with that, their wishes have to come first, as the new partner's status should exceed the status of the Buddy, sometimes that will prove a hard lesson to learn for all three of you.

It often happens that single people have single friends off the dating site, and if you get to know your Buddy really well, you might even be able to recommend someone you know in private life to them, that has happened many times in the past, and some permanent and very happy relationships have come about this way. Also, on more than one occasion people have grown so close to their Buddy they have ended up in very loving relationships with them, realising that the person they trusted the most, was the one they fell for in the end!

TOP TIPS:
- Get close to your Buddy.
- Always do your best for their safety and future happiness.
- Review their favourites with them and make helpful suggestions.
- Take your responsibilities as their Buddy seriously.
- Be there if they need you.
- Remember that one day the relationship will end and be prepared for that.
- Make sure your Buddy knows that when you commit to a new partner, their duties and responsibilities as your Buddy will stop.

People From Overseas

E arlier on in this book I suggested a thirty mile search radius when you first joined a dating site. However many dating sites these days are truly international, and you may have the facility on yours to interact with people from all over the world. Of course this greatly increases your chances of finding a partner, but it also adds a new dimension to your search; what happens if you are contacted by someone from another country, and you really like the look of them? All the advice given so far remains unchanged, you will still need a Buddy, and the way you handle yourself remains unaltered, but now you will need to be aware of time differences, and obviously talking to them on the telephone can become quite expensive, especially for long international calls. If you do decide to search internationally, or you allow your profile to be seen internationally, then get your self a good International 'Phone Plan. It will save you a fortune in call charges.

A simple phrase book for the native language of the country where you seem to have most response from is also worth considering; as is some internet or local library research into its currency, customs and political stability. There are many airlines now offering cheap flights, and there are great deals to be had for the last minute, internet booking traveller.

When I was searching for a partner, a few years ago now, I was contacted by three women overseas. One was from a small state in Africa, one from Russia, and one from Venezuela. If you have not travelled extensively around the world, there is something strange and exotic in chatting to people from a completely different country and culture. The experience of chatting with people from a very different background can be a rewarding one. However, there are unscrupulous persons inhabiting the internet from every country, and once again I say beware, be prepared, and be forewarned.

I was first contacted by the African lady one Friday evening, and after chatting to her for only a little while, she told me that she thought I could be "the one" for her. She announced I was the most handsome man she had ever seen, and she was falling in love with me! Then suddenly she had to go, and simply disappeared.

She reappeared as suddenly as she had vanished the next day, and immediately told me that she had explained our "relationship" to her father, and he would be very pleased to meet me! Then she asked if I would be kind enough to send her the cost of two plane tickets, so that her father and she could come over to meet me.

How does this all sound to you so far? When I looked at some of her pictures, it was apparent to me she was little more than a child, and my internal alarm bells were ringing loud and clear. Scams like this are commonplace, especially from the African continent, and I would strongly urge you to be very wary. Middle aged and elderly western women are also the targets of young African men, who after chatting for a while will inevitably ask for money for a plane ticket to come and see you, or to finance their baby sister's life saving operation, or something else of a like kind. Please do not be persuaded to part with any of your money no matter how plausible the story, I can almost guarantee you will never see it or them again.

I also chatted with a stunningly beautiful lady from Russia, who was also completely swept off her feet by my amazing good looks, and Russian men just didn't understand her like I did, and so on. She got no money either.

The lady from Venezuela seemed to be different. She told me she worked as a lawyer, and loved her job, (that's more like it), and after chatting to her for a few weeks she still had never once asked me for a penny. However, unless I was willing to travel to South America in the near future, or she was willing to come to western Europe, I didn't see much of a future in the relationship, and after a while we simply stopped communicating.

My personal opinion is that it's tricky enough finding a partner in your own country, without adding the extra pressure of a vast distance between you both as well. But once again, this book is for the brave and the romantic at heart, so make up your own mind. Just be extra vigilant when you are contacted by someone from overseas.

TOP TIPS:

- Get yourself a good International Telephone Plan.
- Do some research on the country you get responses from.
- <u>NEVER</u> send money to anyone you have just met.
- Be wary of underage contacts, especially from Africa, the Baltic and the old Soviet Union.
- Understand that it is the western lifestyle which attracts these people more than you!

Accepting, Postponing and Declining

We have assumed up until now that male or female you have been doing all the running. That is to say, you have been contacting potential partners left and right, and chatting with those who responded to you. You may have even been out on dates with a few. But, sooner or later, someone is going to contact you. They will like your picture, have read your profile, and now they want to get to know you better. When someone asks you for a chat, you really only have three basic options open to you, that is to either accept, postpone or decline, simply ignoring the request is rude, and not recommended.

Most people are really quite polite, and don't like to hurt other people's feelings, even if they don't know them. For this reason a lot of people will find declining an invitation extremely difficult. In order to try and lessen the blow, they will start to make excuses and will end up tying themselves in emotional knots, rather than face the issue head on. Also, in order to avoid the abrasive nature of declining, and rather than accept someone they really don't want to talk to, most people will take the safe middle ground and postpone. All they are doing is setting themselves up for exactly the same trauma the next time they log on to the site, as the unwanted caller has now been given hope of a chat in the future. Throughout this book we have declared honesty to be the best policy, and that is also true here. So deal with each new request for an exchange truthfully and directly as soon as it is made.

This section has been written in order to show you how to politely accept, postpone or decline any invitation from anyone, in a firm but still friendly manner.

Accepting

This is the easy part. A simple *"Yes thank you, I would like that."* will work every time.

Postponing

This is the tricky one. Don't use this instead of declining, it will only allow the person to think you really want to talk to them but for a number of reasons cannot do so right now. Therefore they will contact you again the next time they see you, and then you will be in the same position you are right now. Postponing is for people you really *do* want to talk to, but are too busy right now.

"I would like to chat with you, but I am really busy at the moment. I am sorry. Would you contact me again next time, and I will make sure I have the time for a chat, is that OK?"

Or

"I would like to chat with you, but I am really busy at the moment, can you give me (five/ten/fifteen) minutes and I will contact you back? Thanks for being so understanding. We'll have a chat in a little while."

Both of these statements are polite, reasonable and self-explanatory. Almost anyone receiving this type of reply will be quite satisfied with it and willing to wait for you to come back to them. Of course you should always keep your word, and *do* contact them back in the time period you specified. When you contact them back, something like this…

"Hi, sorry about that. I seem to be popular tonight! So, how are you?"

…will prove to them you can keep your promises, you're popular, and you were worth the wait!

Declining

People make such heavy going of this one, when really there is no need. Be polite but firm and friendly, and do not allow someone who is not attractive to you, to waste your time, remember you're paying for your time on the site with your money. If they're wasting your time, they're wasting your money too.

"I am sorry. But you don't fit the type of person I am looking for on here. However, you do have a nice profile, and I wish you all the best of luck!"

If they respond with anything other than a polite goodbye, ignore the message. If they continue to contact you then......

"I have told you I am not interested. Please do not continue to contact me."

These two lines alone will give ninety-nine percent of people the message. The other one percent should not be on dating sites but in therapy. One last message will see them off....

"I have now told you twice. I will not respond to you again. Should you continue to harass me like this I will contact the site and make a formal complaint about you. Good bye."

If you think that is a little too harsh for you then try...

"I have told you that I am not interested. You seem like a nice person, but you are definitely not for me, you are too tall/short. Please do not continue to waste both of our time like this, as I will end up falling out with you, and I do not want to do that. So good luck with your search, and good-bye."

Sooner or later you will find yourself in the predicament of holding several conversations at once. The more simultaneous chats you engage in, the slower will become your responses to each one, regardless of your typing ability; and the shallower each conversation will become, as you simply won't have the time to compose thoughtful or meaningful replies to each person you are in contact with. Consider here that quality must be better than quantity, and set your self a limit to the number you can comfortably handle at once. Remember you are trying to discover if the person you are talking to is the right person for you to spend the remainder of your life with, so it's vitally important to get to know them properly, and you can't do that if the exchanges with them are shallow are meaningless. I never spoke to more than two people at a time, because I liked my chats to be in depth and meaningful; I liked to think about my responses before I sent them, and I just couldn't do that if I was handling too many at once. So if you decide to only talk to two or three at the same time, then make this part of your rule set, and stick to it, by postponing or declining all other requests when you're up to your limit.

TOP TIPS:

- Always try to be friendly but stick to your guns.
- Use the above phrases they are tried and tested.
- If you have to make a complaint, do so, but try to deal with it yourself first.
- Don't postpone when you know you should decline.
- Stick to a small number of simultaneous chats. Go for quality over quantity.

4. ALLOWING THE SITE TO WORK AGAINST YOU

Blocking and Being Blocked

At the end of the previous chapter I recommended that you complain to the site managers as a last resort if someone on the dating site will not leave you alone, after you have told them you are not interested. There is another way which a lot of people prefer. It is quick, simple and straight-forward, that is to "block" them.

Every site has a blocking mechanism available to each and every member. It is simply a way of denying your presence on the site to a specific member; so that should Jack block Jill for instance, then Jill will never know when Jack is on the site, as his profile will not show up on Jill's searches. If she has kept him as a favourite, he will never appear as "live" in her favourites list. The same mechanism exists nowadays on pretty much every instant messaging service as well, and most people will be fairly familiar with the idea.

A word of caution here. Some sites will closely monitor you, and some will simply exclude you altogether if you receive too many blocks in a short space of time, the assumption being that you are becoming a general pest to a number of people. If this happens there is little or no chance of proving your innocence, as there may not even be an appeals procedure in place. Check with the site you join on their exclusion policy, and how they stand on members blocking one another, and if there is a maximum number of times a person may block, or be blocked in a specific period.

A good rule of thumb is to only block someone who will not leave you alone, when you have tried all other reasonable methods to convince them you are not interested.

It is very easy to block someone, all it takes is the press of a button. Because of this you may find you have been blocked by someone who simply didn't like the fact you turned them down! It can be as unfair as that! So be warned. If you use similar phrases as the ones described in the section on accepting, postponing and declining you should be all right; I don't think may people would take a serious offence if you turned them down in a firm but friendly manner. Unjustified blocking tends to occur as a response to hurt feelings; if someone thinks you slighted them in some way they may block you...men react in this way more than women. So when declining please pay special attention to the advice given in the previous chapter.

TOP TIPS:

- Familiarise yourself with the exclusion criteria for the site you are on.
- Only block as a last resort.

Ghost Profiles

L et's suppose you have already met someone on your dating site, and your relationship with them is beginning to blossom into something more meaningful. This often happens with the internet where people feel a very strong bond with another person whom they have never even met face to face. Before you commit to meet them, or perhaps even to travel thousands of miles to another continent to meet them, you might consider finding out if your feelings for them are returned in truth; and if they are going to be really as loyal to you as they profess they are. How to achieve this? One way is to create what has become known as a ghost profile.

A ghost profile is the profile of a person who does not really exist. Perhaps an example will serve to illustrate the point. Mary has been chatting to John for some time now, and John is telling her that she is the only one for him, etc etc. If Mary has never met John, how can she be sure of his feelings towards her, and his real intentions? Mary can decide to test John's fidelity with a ghost profile. In order to do this Mary creates Cindy. Mary joins the site a *second* time, she enters a new username, she enters a completely different set of personal details, and she uploads a photograph of one of her good looking friends who is not on the site. She calls the new profile Cindy, for example. She then writes Cindy's profile, and as Cindy, Mary contacts John. John cannot tell the two women are the same person as the site will not tell him his contact's personal email address, therefore he cannot know Cindy's is the same one as Mary's; all he knows is that an attractive woman called Cindy is interested in talking to him. Now it's up to John. If he flirts with Cindy, and responds to her romantic or sexual suggestions, or agrees to meet Cindy, then Mary knows the truth about her new "friend". If John on the other hand reveals to Cindy that he has made a commitment to Mary, and will see how that works out before he makes any arrangements with anyone else, then Mary will also know the truth about John; and that's how a ghost profile works. The purists amongst you will think this is a scandalous trick, the rest of you will think it's a great idea. Ghost profiles have been created by men who have pretended to be lesbians...and by women trying to catch out cheating lovers. There are many uses for ghost profiles, all of them are devious, and most of them will get you reprimanded by the dating site if you're discovered.

So how do you tell if you're being contacted by a ghost? The truth is you can't, unless they slip up and give the game away. Your only protection from a ghost profile is your own loyalty, honesty and integrity...

Angela from Dating Direct said:

"I was already to move in with Michael. (Name changed). Our relationship on the site had been going from strength to strength over a couple of months, and I felt there was something very special about 'us', and I was sure Michael felt the same way. I heard about the ghost profile thing from a girlfriend who was on another site at the time, and just to keep her quiet, I agreed to try a ghost on Michael. I created Melanie, and used my friend's picture. I created Melanie's profile, consciously making her seem like a trollop. When Melanie contacted Michael I thought he would have told her how committed he was to me, (Angela). I couldn't believe my eyes when the messages which he sent to her came back; it was obvious he was more than willing to meet her. So I arranged a date with Michael as Melanie. I called Michael that night and asked him if we could go out, just to give him one last chance to do the right thing. He told me he was seeing his brother for a drink, and couldn't make it! The rat! He was standing outside the pub waiting for Melanie when I arrived. The pleasure I got from slapping his face and seeing his expression almost made the whole thing worth while. I told him the slap was from both me and Melanie, and I left him to work it out if he could."

Yvonne from Yahoo said:

"*I had been chatting to Marc from Amsterdam for a few weeks. Things had progressed rapidly between us, and he had invited me over from Scotland to spend a couple of weeks with him. I had been looking forward to going, but something was telling me that Marc was not being as honest with me as he should have been. My sister Carol was also on the same site and told me about Ghost Profiles. Carol said she had never used one because she trusted her partner, Ian completely. Carol had met Ian a few months ago on the site, and they were going to resign together. Carol said I should try a Ghost Profile on Marc, and I said to be fair if I tried a Ghost on Marc, then she would have to try the same Ghost on Ian. We agreed to this.*

One night Carol and I got together at my flat, and we created "Suzie" We found a set of pictures of this beautiful girl in a magazine, and we just scanned them onto the computer. We wrote Suzie's profile in about ten minutes, we said she was an English air stewardess, based in Paris and a part-time fashion model. When Suzie was ready we launched her on the site and we had Suzie wink at Marc. I couldn't believe it, Marc replied almost instantly! I was very hurt and offended. Carol consoled me, and we continued to chat to Marc as Suzie, until I was left with no illusions about my Dutch boyfriend.

Carol was so sympathetic, but I thought she seemed a little smug too. She had always disliked Marc. I said it was time to test Ian. Suzie contacted Ian, and a few moments passed, nothing came back. Suzie contacted Ian again, still nothing.

'I told you Ian was going to be faithful to me' Said Carol.

I had to admit I was very hurt and upset. My sister's boyfriend had proved to be more loyal to her, than mine was to me. We were about to shut the site down and go out for a drink to talk about what had happened, when an email came through from the site to Suzie. Ian said he was sorry he didn't reply straight away as he was looking up flights to Paris on the internet and he could fly over to see Suzie tomorrow morning!

We dumped both our boyfriends the very next day. I feel sad that we were taken in so much, and sad we both lost relationships; but Suzie showed us what Rats we were dating, and we will always be grateful to her for that."

TOP TIPS:

- Create a ghost profile if you think you have met the "One" before you commit
- Only do it if you feel you just need to be reassured.
- Remember, when you launch a Ghost Profile, you may discover some unpleasant truths, you may regret doing it. Only create a Ghost if you are willing to accept the consequences!

Cyber Sex

B ecause relationships on dating sites tend to become more intense much more rapidly than they would in the "real" or outside world, the issue of sex will often arise very early on. You may have contacted or been contacted by someone you like, and you begin to chat with them through the whispering system on the site. If you have followed the guidelines provided previously, you will already have at least something in common with this person, and there is likely to be a degree of mutual attraction already present. So you like each other. As you become more and more familiar as your chatting continues, sooner or later the conversation will take on a sexual dimension, this is almost inevitable. Everyone will have their own comfort zone and boundaries here, and it is the purpose of this section to prepare you for what is to happen, and to ensure you are able to handle it when it does. Remember always that it is *your* membership, *your* time, *your* money and *your* life, therefore you should be in total control of all of it.

Let's face it, when the subject of sex arises, either you are going to be comfortable with it, or you are not. No-one wants to sound like a prude these days, and often people will go along with an uncomfortable or embarrassing sequence of exchanges rather than put a stop to it and appear to be "immature" or somehow sexually repressed. This is confused thinking. Take control of what is happening to you, and if a boundary has been crossed you need to take action. Everyone's boundaries will be set at different points, and what is embarrassing to one, will be exciting to another; it is your choice.

If you are comfortable discussing sex over the instant messaging system, then go with it, the whole point of joining the site in the first place was to meet a romantically and sexually compatible partner anyway, but there are comfort limits for everyone. If you are not comfortable with the way the exchanges are going, then you need to be able to steer the boat back into calmer waters. If that is the case, then try something like this.

"I really like talking to you, and I do want to get to know you better, but I am a little uncomfortable with the way this conversation is going right now. I am not really ready for this, and I would prefer it if we talked about something else for now. Is that OK?"

By producing a well thought out objection in this way you achieve three things simultaneously. Firstly, you tell them that you are interested in them, you like them and do want to continue to explore your blossoming relationship. Secondly, you tell them you have certain standards that you are going to enforce. You're not a prude, and perhaps sometime in the future you might be willing to become intimate with them in this way, but not today. Thirdly, that you have a mind of your own, and in any relationship which does become serious between you in the future, you will play an equal part, and make some of the decisions. Believe me, you will get more respect instantly by taking control this way, and they are more, not less likely to want to keep you as a favourite, and to continue to exchange with you, only now it's on your terms.

Of course sex is not the only subject that makes some people uncomfortable. You can use the above objection for *any* subject that you wish to change. Some people for instance are very politically active, others hate discussing politics. Some people have a religious affiliation which they will want to share with others, and some people are not religiously minded at all, and do not like to discuss such topics. Whenever any exchange breeches a limit for you, or begins to make you feel less than comfortable, wherever that is, use the above objection and make suitable changes. It does raise the question though, if you are objecting to subjects frequently with the same person, can they really be right future partner for you?

TOP TIPS:
- Don't allow an uncomfortable conversation to go unchallenged.
- Be polite, firm and friendly in your challenges.
- Don't be afraid to take control when you need to, be assured, they will respect you more for it.

How Fast Is Too Fast?

Everyone has an emotional speed limit, what's yours? If you met someone you really liked in a bar, for instance, how much time would have to pass before you would sleep with them? Or how many dates would it take before you felt an emotional attraction so strong you wanted to make a romantic commitment to them? The answer to these questions will be different for everyone. Some people have no problem with having sex with a person hours after meeting them, for others it may take months. The point is that whatever figure of time you have in mind, you can safely divide that by two when you're on a dating site! As has previously been stated everything happens much faster here, it's very easy to get carried away with some gorgeous, sexy new favourite, and the danger is that you find yourself in over your head before you even realise what's happened. I know of a case where marriage was proposed, and accepted within one hour of first contact. I have no idea if they're still together, personally I doubt it.

If sex is what you're looking for, then you really are on the wrong site; there are plenty of sites around for no-strings sexual encounters, and you're also reading the wrong book! This book has been carefully put together over a long period of time, after extensive research, in order to assist genuine people who are looking for lifetime partners. It has been written to help them avoid the pitfalls, and to show them some tried and tested methods that really work. This is for partner seekers, not sex seekers, and I make no apologies for that.

So, if you find yourself suddenly in a whirlwind romance that appears out of control, if you're going too fast too soon, then this is where your Buddy comes back in. If you have followed the previous steps already outlined, your Buddy will have checked out this person's profile, and discussed them with you; but your Buddy doesn't know them personally, and therefore is more detached and objective than you. Your Buddy should be able to provide you with a sobering voice here, and you really should listen to them.

If you find yourself going too fast too soon, then just slow down....take some time out and give yourself a break from the site, stay away for a few days, it will still be there when you go back; give yourself time to resettle down emotionally, and time to think. Remember what you are trying to achieve here. You are looking to build a permanent, solid and loving relationship which will last long into the future, and all that takes time.

You may not realise it, but the person you have suddenly become involved with may also feel that things are going too fast, but is reluctant to tell you so. Good, honest communication is vital here. Don't be afraid to state your case. If you find yourself in this situation and want to cool things down a bit, then try this.

"I can't believe we have come so far so soon, this is not really like me, and I feel a little out of control right now. Do you feel the same? I haven't changed my mind at all about developing this with you, and seeing where it goes, I just want to take it forward at a slower pace, is that ok?"

If the new favourite has what they used to call "honourable intentions" towards you, then they should be fine with this. If not, then you have discovered something early about them before it was too late.

John from Online Dating says:

"I met this lovely girl and we just clicked right away. It was magical. We both just knew that we were made for each other. But it all happened so fast it was scary. I felt that I was losing control of what was happening to me. When I said this to Anne she said she had felt the same way but didn't want to tell me as she thought I might lose interest in her. Nothing could have been further from the truth. We slowed things right down, and started off again at a much

slower pace. We have been together now for eight months and have discussed getting engaged sometime next year."

TOP TIPS:

- Don't exceed your own emotional speed limit, crashes are painful!
- Don't be afraid to state your case, if you need to slow down tell them!
- Never forget to involve your Buddy, they are more objective than you!

Taking "No" For An Answer

Everyone likes to be liked. When we know that someone likes us, we tend to like them back; unfortunately, it's not possible for everyone to like everyone else, the human race just doesn't work that way, and sooner or later, someone is going to turn you down flat! Bump!

Maybe they didn't like your picture. Maybe they didn't find a connection in your profile. Maybe you're too young or too old for them. Maybe they're just about to make a commitment to another person they met before you, who knows? For whatever the reason they have said, "No" and they meant it. Yes, it hurts, the ego gets bruised and we feel a little foolish or embarrassed. That's ok. Retain your dignity at all times, and *please* don't ask them for the reason why they don't want to talk to you, being on the receiving end of such a question is terrible...just wish them good luck and move away. You can always call up your Buddy later and tell them you have been turned down by the most insensitive, shallow, short-sighted, brainless fool on the whole internet, and your Buddy will agree with you! Then when you're done complaining to your Buddy about something they had nothing to do with in the first place, you can go straight back onto the site and talk to someone else.

Remember we only know about people what their profiles tell us. There is so much more to everyone, but our decisions are based on only a very limited amount of information, so don't take the rejection personally. In reality, they haven't turned you down as a person at all, they can't because they don't know you! All they have done is decline the *opportunity* to know you, and that's not the same thing at all, that's just the way you should look at it. Think of it as their loss, not yours, and move on.

Sarah from U Date says:

"I used to feel upset when someone I approached didn't really want to talk to me. Now I realise that's just silly. I think of it in terms of a house party. If you walk into a crowded room where you don't know many people what do you do? You 'mingle', you say 'Hi' to people here and there, some will spend time with you, and other's won't, that's ok. I talk to the ones who want to talk to me, and pass by the one's who don't. It's easy and simple when you think of it

*like that. You're just saying hi to a crowd of people. It's up
to them after that."*

TOP TIPS:

- Don't take the rejection personally, they don't know you!
- Don't harass them after the rejection, delete them from your favourites list, if they're in there, forget about them, and move on.
- Unload on your Buddy if you want to, that's one of the reasons they're there!
- Never ask someone who has turned you down for a reason why, it's demeaning for you, (it's like begging) and it embarrasses them. Retain your dignity at all times.
- If *you* are ever asked "why?" Tell them you're involved with someone else and are not accepting new contacts. That spares their feelings and gives you an easy way out.

Obsession and Addiction

I f you have never been a member of a dating site, you might find it amusing to learn there are dating site junkies out there. These are people who have lost sight of the original reason as to why they became members, (to find a life partner), and simply continue to log on, night after night, chatting to everyone in sight, and hardly ever meeting anyone. These people have become addicted to the rush of chatting up or hitting on strangers in a safe environment. Whilst no one would deny this practice is great fun, it does tend to leave you nowhere in the end.

I went through such a phase myself, it tends to occur when you first become a full member, where I was coming in from work, and before I had even had time to take my jacket off, was logging on to my favourite dating site to see if anyone had left me a message in my absence. Then I would spend the next five hours, chatting with my favourites, and meeting new people until it was time to go to bed. The next night would be spent in exactly the same way. I was lucky though, I managed to somehow realise that the original point of becoming a member was not to chat aimlessly for hours with friends, but to arrange dates with people, so I could eventually find a partner. Once that realisation occurred to me, I began to use my time on the site more effectively, and started to curtail how long I was on there; I cut my visits down from every night, to every other night, and made a rule to stay on there for two hours per visit, maximum. This allowed me to also have a life offline.

I met some really nice people on these sites, and some of them are still friends with me, even though both they and I have left the sites after having found great partners. But this is not always the case, and I personally know a number of very attractive people, both women and men who continue to frequent these sites, year after year, not because they can't get a date, but because they can't give up the site itself! I know one man who has had several partners, great women all of them, but they couldn't tolerate him continuing to chat with other women online when he was supposed to be going out with them.

It's great to be hit on by someone really attractive, our ego takes a total boost, and the feeling we receive can become addictive. Here is the real danger of dating sites; not that we will become unsuccessful in finding dates, but that we will become too successful in finding favourites! This happens to millions of people the whole world over, and I have dedicated the last section to this problem, *Quitting Together*. But for now, we need a way, a mechanism to keep us on track; we don't all want to become dating site junkies do we? We want to succeed in our original aim of finding a great partner and then leaving the site. The dating site is a means to an end therefore, not an end in itself.

If you find yourself falling into the above trap, spending a very large amount of your free time on the site, and just chatting, then you need to take a break. There is a life outside the internet, and you need to go and find it.

Limit the nights you spend on the site, find other things to do on those spare nights, and limit the amount of time you spend on the site on the nights you have allocated for it. If you decrease the time you spend on there, you force yourself to become more constructive with the time you do have. So don't just chat to friends, arrange dates with them! Arrange dates with all your favourites, and make your time productive!

Melina from asiafriendfinder said:

"I joined my dating site about a year ago. I have made some great friends, and it wasn't until my annual membership came up for renewal this year that I realised a year had flown by! I have had a wonderful time, but I haven't met anyone seriously yet, because I spend all my

time chatting to my favourites for hours nearly every night; it has become like a very intimate social club. We tell each other about our days at work, and our lives, then we all say goodnight about eleven and go to bed. I realised that was not why I joined the site. So now I spend more time searching for a nice date than I do chatting with my friends. And I have also started to see some of my favourites at the weekends, this is a much better strategy, and I feel my time is being spent much more wisely now."

TOP TIPS:
- Remember why you joined in the first place!
- Be productive with your time.
- Arrange a date with a favourite every time you are on the site if you can.
- Contact three new strangers every time you go on the site.
- Ask out all your favourites.
- Limit both the amount of times you visit the site each week, and the time you spend on each visit.

Scams

As has already been mentioned, there are unscrupulous people on dating sites just as there are in every other walk of life. Because these people have scant regard for human feeling, they see internet daters as being easy targets. They assume people on dating sites are lonely, and they are also often susceptible to a bit of totally insincere flattery. They are seen as being comparatively wealthy, (divorced, or widowed women), and therefore an easy touch. The awful truth is that often they are right. Middle-aged women who have come out of a long-term marriage, either through divorce or a husband's death, are often quite financially solvent and stable. It is this group who are most at risk from the internet fortune hunter, closely followed by middle-aged men, who have successful careers and think a lovely girl of eighteen really means it when she tells him he is the most handsome man she has ever seen!

The sharks are out there, they can sound extremely plausible, and their stories would break your heart, even if they were true! So let's look at a few typical examples:

The Female Target

Let's call her Agnes. She's typically between 40 and 50, has been left a decent amount of money through either death or divorce, probably owns real estate, perhaps her own home, and has a tidy amount in the bank. Typically she lives in Western Europe, Canada or the United States. She isn't that hard to spot if you know what to look for. Agnes has been on her own now for five years. She decided to join a dating site for curiosity more than anything else. She has never heard of the Buddy Safety System, and she will happily chat to anyone who contacts her. Agnes is a nice lady, and she's lonely.

One day a very handsome young man, let's say he's in his early thirties, contacts Agnes. He tells her she must have been a film star when she was a little younger; because she's still beautiful now, and he thinks her profile is wonderful, he's been waiting all his life to meet her. Agnes can hardly catch her breath…

Agnes and this young man get on like a house on fire, they chat for hours each night over the instant messaging system on the dating site, and after a few weeks, Agnes is in love.

Then very suddenly, one day he fails to appear. Agnes wonders what could have happened to him, she sits for hours watching her screen at home, waiting for him to log on, but he doesn't arrive. Agnes finally goes to bed that night bitterly disappointed and perplexed. He doesn't show the next day either, and Agnes becomes concerned. She starts to ask herself some searching questions: What if he had an accident? What if he's found someone younger? What if he's changed his mind about their future together? Poor Agnes is now distraught with anxiety and worry.

Suddenly he appears again. He professes his undying love for Agnes, she is mad with excitement and relief, and then he tells her he can never ever see her again. Agnes's world explodes into fragments. He tells her that he has been at the hospital, where his little sister has been diagnosed with brain cancer. He tells Agnes that the life saving operation will cost his family $20,000 and he can never see her again because he will have to go away to work for a man so he can raise the money....He tells Agnes how much he loves her, but he can't let his little sister die....Oh let us not continue with this story, we both know exactly where it's going don't we?

Of course, good and kind Agnes pays for the operation by the BACS system of international electronic money transfer, and neither the young man, nor her money are ever seen again.

If you are reading this and wondering how Agnes could have been so gullible, please don't! Agnes was truly in love, she had no Buddy to defend her when she was not thinking straight, and she was lonely to begin with. It may surprise you to learn that this scam has been successful *thousands* of times, and continues to be practiced today in your country!

Sometimes our young man has a different tale to tell. Let's suppose during one of their conversations the topic of homes and lifestyles arose. Agnes sends this young man a picture of her beautiful home, the young man knows it's a lot better than his place, and he would really like to live there...so he proposes marriage. If Agnes accepts, he will clean her out when the marriage ends, which it will once he gets leave to stay in Agnes' country, or when her money runs out, which ever comes first.

The Male Target

Meet Henry. He's a businessman who has a bald head, an expanding waistline and an even more expanding bank balance. His wife of 30 years died two years ago, and Henry misses her every single day. Henry can be any age, but typically, he's around 50. Henry joined the dating site because he's lonely, and that makes him an easy target for someone with the right approach.

One day Henry is contacted on the site by Amanda. She is beautiful, sexy, and half Henry's age, but Henry thinks that doesn't matter. Henry thinks Amanda is not only fabulous to look at; she's also a fantastic judge of character, because she told him she is tired of immature little boys, and is looking for a real man. Henry will do just about anything for Amanda.

If Henry doesn't have a Buddy right now he's in trouble. His ego will blind him to the truth, and sooner or later Amanda will ask for a 'plane ticket, the money for an operation, (or some other desperate cause in Amanda's life), or she will ask Henry if he's really serious about her…the characters in the play vary from production to production, but the plots are all the same, and they all end in tragedy.

Three weeks after Henry marries Amanda and she has citizenship of his country, she will leave him high and dry, and his bank balance will be a lot smaller than it was before he met her.

It is never a good idea to generalise about large groups of people, but the facts are that people in poorer countries, the African sub-continent, the Baltic States and the old Soviet Union do have a chance of a much improved lifestyle if they marry someone from the Western World; the United States, the United Kingdom, most of the Western European countries, Australia, New Zealand and Canada.

If you are on a dating site, and you allow international contacts, and you happen to live in one of the "target countries", please be careful. Consult your Buddy on every contact, especially on those from people who live in one of the mentioned areas and are a lot younger than contacts you would normally expect to receive.

The British Government has produced a website to give information about this, it is useful for everyone on a dating site whether they live in the UK or not. The British Government department is The Office of Fair Trading, their web address is:

"http://www.oft.gov.uk/"

Once on the site go to Scams, then Online Dating. Although everything mentioned there has already been stated during the course of this book, but it might help to drive the message home if you see it printed by a government source.

MAIN TARGET COUNTRIES	MAIN PREDATOR COUNTRIES
AUSTRALIA	ALBANIA
AUSTRIA	AZERBIJAN
CANADA	BOSNIA
DENMARK	CROATIA
FINLAND	KHAZAKSTAN
FRANCE	LITHUANIA
GERMANY	MOROCCO
HOLLAND	MOZAMBIQUE
IRELAND	NIGER
NEW ZEALAND	ROMANIA
SWEDEN	RUSSIA
SWITZERLAND	SERBIA
UNITED KINGDOM	TUNISIA
UNITED STATES	UZBEKISTAN

I have said before that it is never a good idea to generalise about groups of people, and that remains the case. I have travelled throughout most of what I have disparagingly called the "Predator" countries on the above list, and have found those citizens to be charming, charitable and very hospitable on many occasions. However, the fact remains that most of the internet scams around today originate on this list, and the targets of those scams are on the first list, so I make no apologies for including both lists here, as it is the purpose of this book to protect, warn, educate and guide its readership.

TOP TIPS:

- If you live in a target country, be wary of younger, attractive contacts from the specified areas.
- Consult your Buddy on every new international contact, and listen to them
- Never send money to a contact, regardless of what story they tell you, especially when you have never met them.
- If you are suspicious about them, report them to the site.

5. TAKING THINGS FURTHER

Instant Messaging Facilities

By now you must be aware of the dating site's internal instant messaging facility. This is the way potential partners will make first contact with you, most often. You can tell a lot about a person by the way they write and respond to whispers. If a person takes an unusual time to respond to a message you have sent, they may be having several conversations at once, and this will explain the time delay in replying to you.

When you have been chatting with a contact on the site for a while, they will usually ask for either your telephone number or email address. It is probably a good idea to chat to them for a while on an external and universal instant messaging system before you give them your telephone number.

A lot of people use msn these days, and similar services are available to everyone; pictures can be sent through the IM system very quickly and easily, and often the early internet daters will swap photographs and funny stories off the site in this way. It is harmless fun, and it moves the budding relationship on to the next stage. If there is a darker or unpleasant side to the person you have just met, then it is more likely to become apparent now. Instant Messaging allows the user to effectively block an unwelcome contact with no more effort than pressing a button. If they do have a darker side, find it now rather than later, and simply block them.

Instant Messaging can be a lot of fun, and if you spend some time chatting with potential dates in this way you should be able to find out a great deal about them before you agree to see them face to face. Another bonus of this way of doing things is that when you eventually decide you do want to meet them, the date should go very well, simply because by now you will know so much more about them you will have lots in common to talk about.

Chatting on an IM system can be fast and furious. The questions, comments and responses fly back and forth at a very rapid pace sometimes, especially when you are both chatting about something you both share an interest in. Do pause, and read what you have just written before you send it, sometimes you will want to correct grammatical and spelling errors, or change a word or two before sending the message.

Webcams have become very popular over the last few years. They are cheap and easy to install and will allow you to actually see the person you are talking to, and of course they can also see you, providing you both have a mutually compatible camera. Using a webcam in conjunction with an IM system off the site can be great fun for both of you, and it can help develop a new relationship by adding an extra dimension to your chats. This will allow you to *see* your favourite, as well as message them in real time; the exercise will suddenly become more personal for both of you. You will be able to see a at least a part of their home environment, and you can gain even more information about them. If the picture on their profile is not an accurate one, then the webcam will betray their secret, so to speak. Watching someone move, even if are they only sitting at a keyboard will add something to what you already know about them. You can also watch their natural reactions carefully when you ask them a question, so that it is easier to gauge their true feelings in this way. It is harder to lie successfully when you are being watched, than when you are not. Of course when intimacy enters the mix, (as it will), and you are both on a webcam, there is the temptation to perform for the camera in a sexually provocative way, which might not be something you would consider doing under any other circumstances.

Think carefully before you proceed!

Exchanges in this medium are often intimate in nature, and can feel very sexually stimulating. I would repeat here the advice given in the section, *Cyber Sex*. If you are comfortable with the way the exchanges are going, no problem, enjoy it. If you feel you are getting out of your depth, then challenge the flow, and take action. We have already discussed ways in which you can do this.

TOP TIPS:

- Never be in a rush to meet someone face to face, get to know them through the IM system first. Getting to know them this way will allow the first date to go smoother anyway.
- Think of the IM system as simply the next stage in developing your relationship.
- Use a webcam if you both have one. But think carefully if you are asked to "perform" for the camera in a way that makes you feel uncomfortable.
- Check grammar and spelling, and read what you have just written before you hit the send button.

E-mails

T he art of writing a romantic letter is fast becoming a thing of the past. In my opinion this is a terrible shame. There are few nicer things you can receive through your computer than a well written, thoughtful, lengthy love letter. It can be saved and re-read time and time again, and only the email facility will allow you to achieve this.

Think of this as the next stage on from the IM system of communication with your new contact. The email will not replace the instant message, nor was it ever intended to, but it does *compliment* it beautifully. Use the IM when you are both logged on at the same time for a chat in real time; but when you have a few moments to yourself, send them an e-letter.

You could make it as sentimental as you want to, or as straight forward. You could begin by simply telling them how much you enjoy your evening chats with them, and you look forward to the time when you can meet them in person. If you are writing to them through an external emailing system off the dating site, like yahoo or hotmail for instance, you could attach a photograph of yourself to the email and send them together. Or perhaps a picture of your favourite place, a restaurant for instance, where you would like to take them when you eventually decide to have your first date.

Spend some time and put some effort into the letter, it will pay dividends, as people like to feel they are thought of as being special; and by spending time in composing a romantic and thoughtful letter, you are investing a small amount of your spare time in them. It is a nice thought, and people do appreciate the gesture.

There are also a few really good e-card sites around. These are sites where you can send someone a birthday, or anniversary card through the e-mail system of your own computer. Check them out, *Blue Mountain* is one I use, as I like the choice of card they have on offer.

Gordon from meetic said:

"I first saw Angela about six months ago on the site, and sent her a wink before I had even read her profile. I thought she was beautiful in her photographs, but she ignored the contact. I winked a few more times to her over the next few weeks, but she just made no response at all. I didn't want to pester her, and I was just about to give up, when I thought about writing to her properly. I had previously

toyed with the idea of whispering to her, but as she had never replied to a wink from me, I thought she might not want to chat to me either. I thought if I could explain a little about myself in a letter, she might just read it. I spend the next three days writing this letter; I wrote about how nice I thought she looked, and how I hoped we could get to know one another. I even composed a short poem and included that. I was really nervous about mailing it to her, but when the time came I just thought that if she doesn't reply to this then she really doesn't want to know, and I won't approach her again. I was on the site the next day after I sent the email letter and she whispered to me. We began to chat like we had known each other for years, and we became very close over the following couple of months. Now we have had several dates together which have all gone very well, and we're talking about the future. Angela says she thought the letter was so nice and romantic that she had to talk to me after she read it. She told me she never replies to winks"

Angela from meetic said:

"I had received a couple of winks from Gordon, he looked nice, but I don't reply to winks. If a man winked at me in the street I wouldn't go and over and talk to him, so why should I on a dating site? And I don't like to make the first approach anyway; I am still a bit old fashioned like that, I prefer the man to make the first effort at a conversation, and I don't call a simple wink an effort. He could have sent dozens of winks to different women, they're so easy to do,

they don't mean anything to me. I waited for him to whisper to me, but nothing came, so I thought he must have moved on to someone else. Then suddenly I had this beautiful email from him. It was a really lovely letter. He wasn't full of himself, like a lot of men on the site are; he was gentle and charming, and he sent me a beautiful poem. I read it over and over, and decided then that I would talk to him when I saw him on the site next time. I simply whispered to Gordon that I really loved the poem and thanked him for the effort it must have taken him, and I appreciated it. We got chatting, and we talk every night now. We have met a couple of times and I am willing to give this relationship a chance, I think it could work, but it's still early days yet, but I must admit, I am hopeful."

TOP TIPS:

- Spend some time in composing a good love letter, you do not have to write it all at once, you can save the letter as you go along, and send it when you have finished revising it. Do use the spell checker at the end.
- Send a photograph with it, one of yourself, or a picture of a nice place you would like to take them when you first meet.
- Send them an e-card, just for the fun of it.

Text Messaging

There are really only two stages left to go through before you meet them face to face; this section and the next one, texting them and calling them. It really makes no difference which way around you do this.

In a way, texts are the direct opposite of e-mailing. Text messages tend to be very brief, heavily abbreviated, completely without manners, normal social etiquette or even good grammatical language. It's like receiving a telegram from a robot in most cases, and we tend to carelessly reply in the same casual fashion. But that's ok as everyone does it. Texts are great for sending brief notes, but with a little imagination they can be fun too.

All languages real or made up evolve with both usage and the passage of time. Text Speak is no different, and by the time you read this the following list will already have some of its items replaced. But for now here is a very short, and by no means comprehensive list of the kind of thing you can expect when you start to text. Of course it's much more fun to make up your own codes with someone, that way you can make the message as intimate as you like and if anyone else sees it they wouldn't know what it meant.

Carole from Udate said:

"I used to send my ex-partner CW2UUL8R" (can't wait to undress you later).

"It really made the journey home much more exciting!"

Text Speak
ASL Age, sex, location?
ABT2 About to
AFAIC As far as I'm concerned
AFAIK As far as I know
ALOL Actually laughing out loud
AML All my love
ASLMH Age, sex, location, music, hobbies?
ATST At the same time
AWOL Absent without leave
AYK As you know
AYSOS Are you stupid or something
AYTMTB And you're telling me this because?

B4 Before
B4N Bye for now
BBT Be back tomorrow
BRB Be right back
BTW By the way
BW Best wishes
BYKT But you knew that

CID Consider it done
CSL Can't stop laughing
CYL See you later
CYT See you tomorrow

DGA Don't go anywhere
DIKU Do I know you?
DLTM Don't lie to me

FEAA For ever and always
FF Friends forever

GBH Great big hug
GG Good game
GL Good luck
GR8 Great
GTG Got to go

HAK Hugs and kisses

ILU I love you
IM Instant message
IMHO In my humble opinion
IMO In my opinion
IMS I am sorry
IOH I'm out of here
JK Just kidding

KEWL Cool
KISS Keep it simple stupid

L8R Later
LMAO Laughing my ass off
LOL Laughs out loud

M8 Mate
MSG Message

N1 Nice one
NE1 Anyone?
NMP Not my problem
NOYB None of your business
NP No problem
NUFF Enough said

OMDB Over my dead body
OMG Oh my gosh
ONNA Oh no, not again
OOTO Out of the office
OT Off topic
OTT Over the top

PLS Please
PM Personal message
POOF Goodbye

QL Quit laughing
QT Cutie

RBTL Reading between the lines
ROLF Rolling on the floor laughing
ROTFLMAO Rolling on the floor laughing my ass
off

SMEM Send me an email
SMIM Send me an instant message
SOHF Sense of humour failure
STR8 Straight
SYS See you soon

TAH Take a hike
TBC To be continued
TFH Thread from hell
TGIF Thank God it's Friday
THX Thanks
TM Trust me
TOM Tomorrow
TTFN Ta ta for now
TTG Time to go
TVM Thank you very much

VM Voice mail

WC Who cares?
WF Way fun
WFM Works for me
WTG Way to go
WYP What's your problem?
WYWH Wish you were here

XOXO Hugs and kisses

ZZZ Sleeping, bored

TOP TIPS:
- Texts are fun, and they have their place, but don't use them instead of e-mails
- Have fun inventing your own codes with your new favourite!

Calling Them

S ome people become very nervous about the idea of calling up someone to ask them for a date. Traditionally, it is the men who have always done the asking, but dating sites are changing all that, and online courtships have their own etiquette, and it's perfectly normal for a woman to make the first call. Nervousness should not be so much of an issue here, as you have already chatted with them on the IM system, either through the dating site itself, or on one of the external services like msn, or yahoo for instance.

So the conversation doesn't sag in the middle, make a few notes before you call them. Recall the whispered conversations you have already had with them, and jot down on a piece of paper some bullet points so you can bring them up as a fresh topic when you talk to them.

It is best if they are expecting your call. You can arrange the time and date to call when they give you their 'phone number when they're whispering to you.

Begin the conversation by telling them it's great to hear their voice at last, and then go from there. It is strange how hearing someone's voice brings their character alive. Up until this point you have only exchanged written messages in whatever form they have taken; IM exchanges, emails or texts. By adding their voice to the mix, you add a new dimension to your impression of them as a person, and suddenly they become less remote, and more real somehow. Asking for their telephone number shouldn't be an ordeal if you've already been chatting with them for some time.

"We seem to be getting on well together, don't we? I would like to hear your voice and speak to you. Would it be OK for me to call you?"

If they say they aren't ready, or decline for another reason, don't be offended, it is their choice after all.

"OK, no problem, we can forget that idea then, so where were we...?"

Just accept their decision with good humour, and resume your former conversation with them on IM. Don't make a big deal out of it. If they do give you the number, then...

"That's great, I'm looking forward to speaking with you, shall I call right now?"

You should have lots to chat about, and the call should be exciting and fun. Don't rush into asking them to meet you, leave that to the end; enjoy chatting with them first, if you are still interested in meeting them after you have spent some time listening to what they have to say instead of reading it, then press ahead for a meeting.

"...we seem to be able to talk to each other very easily, it would be great to meet you. Would you like that?"

Once they have agreed to meet you, suggest a safe meeting place in full public view. If you are going to have a meal together give them the name, address and telephone number of the restaurant, the time and date of the meeting. Tell them what type of restaurant it is, and suggest a dress code. For a first date try to go for "smart casual" nothing too formal. Ask them to call you and tell you when they are leaving for the date.

If on the other hand, you suddenly change your mind, and decided that for whatever reason you no longer wish to meet them face to face; something they have said has put you off, you don't like their accent, they seem totally different now that you have added their voice to the mix, then let the conversation end naturally, say good-bye and hang up.

"...well, I have to go now. It was nice chatting with you again. Bye bye."

For the purposes of the next section we will assume you have spoken successfully to them on the telephone, you still like them, and you have arranged to meet them...so let's prepare for your date.

TOP TIPS:

- Make sure they are expecting the call
- Before you call have notes prepared on what to say.
- Discuss things you like in their profile and recap on previous whispers
- Continue with your conversation naturally if they decline the opportunity for you to call them. Don't be hurt or offended, it's their choice, respect that.
- Arrange the date at the end of your call, not at the beginning

Meeting For The First Time

S o, here we are! This is what it has all been about. If you have followed the advice in the previous section, you have given your date the time, day, address and telephone number of the restaurant, (if applicable). You have suggested a dress code for the evening, and you have asked them to call you when they were leaving, so you know they are still coming. As soon as you had done all that, you very sensibly called up your Buddy and gave them the same information, including your date's username, and real name from the site. You asked your Buddy to call fifteen or twenty minutes after the meeting time, and you have a vocal signal in place with your Buddy to let them know the way you're feeling. This is all standard preparation which you undertake for <u>every</u> date you have from the site.

I am assuming you are meeting for a meal. Of course that may not be the case. Whatever you have decided to do for your first date, whether it is simply for a cup of coffee, a trip around a museum, or a day shopping, there is a golden rule to follow.

<u>Make sure you arrange to meet in a well-lit public place, and stay in well-lit public areas for the whole of the time you are together.</u>

So, let's assume you have decided to go for a meal. You're standing outside the restaurant, and suddenly, there they are! You should be able to instantly recognise them from their profile photograph, if you don't, something is wrong and you need to know why they look different. Everything in their profile should be a true representation of the person, if it's not, then you need to hear an alarm bell ringing in your mind early on. You need to know *why* there is a difference

If their profile says they are six feet tall and they are shorter than that, be blunt with them, they have deceived you and everyone else who has agreed to meet them.

"You've lost a little height! Have you been unwell recently?" Is a good one.

Let's assume you see them walking towards you, and you just know it's ok. So far so good. A big hug is a natural and great way to start off. After all, it's not like you are complete strangers any more. The feeling you will get is something akin to running into an old friend whom you haven't seen for a long time. But keep in the back of your mind that they really are *not* an old friend, you've only just met them.

Now you're in the restaurant. From here on in treat the date like a very informal job interview. That makes it sound terribly unromantic, it need not be, but an interview is exactly what a first date really is!

Imagine you were looking to employ someone for a job you needed to be filled, you would want to know they were the right person with the right qualities to fulfil your needs, and that you would be able to enjoy working with them, right? Well, the job on offer is nothing less than your future, full time life partner! When will you interview someone for a more important position than that? Make sure they measure up!

It's not just sexual compatibility you need to think about. Life involves living together 24/7, so you need to be comfortable eating with them, walking down the street, sharing a laugh, paying bills, going to the shops, and everything else that comprises a modern shared life.

How are they conducting themselves in public? Do their table manners match yours, and do you care? If you don't care, then it doesn't matter what they eat like, but if you do care, are they able to eat in public without embarrassing you? If they can't, it would be much easier to find someone who can, than to try and retrain this one.

If your Buddy calls on time, fifteen or twenty minutes into the interview, you should be able to give the go or stop signal. After twenty minutes you should really know how you feel about this date, and if you want to continue with it or not. First impressions count for a lot, and I would always advise you to go with yours.

If you're not impressed, don't be generous and give them more time, dates are not like wine, they don't improve with age. If you're not impressed right now, you won't be later on, so make up your mind, quit while you're ahead and put it down to experience. If you are impressed, then continue to follow your instincts for a far as they will take you. Enjoy the date for it's own sake, and at the end of it tell them you are looking forward to chatting to them again on the site. Don't make any kind of romantic commitment to them on the first date, you have the rest of your favourites list to interview yet!

When it's over, call your Buddy and let them know you're ok.

TOP TIPS:
- Make sure your Buddy knows all the details about your coming date.
- Arrange stop and go signals with your Buddy before hand
- Give all the details about the venue to your date and suggest a dress code.
- Listen to your first impressions when you first see them

- Treat the date like a job interview, but not formally like one, but do ask some searching questions.
- Make a decision when your Buddy calls
- Enjoy the date if you can, but do not make a commitment at the end of it.
- Call your Buddy and let them know you're ok when its over.

Safety First

A word before we move on. The assumption throughout this book is that you are interested in developing a permanent relationship through a dating site, and all advice is geared towards that assumption. If however, you are simply seeking no-strings sexual encounters, then this book is not for you, nor are dating sites. There are many sites across the net which cater for sex only meetings, and they are readily available to anyone over eighteen. If that is what you are seeking, then the only part of this book that will apply to you is the *Buddy Safety System*, and I would strongly urge you to put such a system firmly in place before your next encounter.

Almost all the problems people experience due to dating site meetings going wrong occur because basic personal safety has been ignored. This advice is good for men as well as women, and this section is really a recap of everything we said before, but it can't be said too many times, and for ease of reference we've gathered it all here in one place.

TOP TIPS:

- Make sure you have a Buddy in place <u>BEFORE</u> you agree to your first date with someone you have met on a dating site.
- Have pre-arranged signal codes worked out with your Buddy before you see anyone. This includes stop and go signals, and a signal asking them to call back in ten more minutes.
- Never give out your personal email address or telephone number to someone you have only just met as a first contact, that comes much later.
- Never give out your home address to anyone you meet on the dating site, until you have had several dates with them and are very sure of them.
- Consult with your Buddy before and after each date
- Be wary of younger contacts you receive from overseas, especially if you happen to live in one of the "target countries"
- <u>NEVER</u> send money to anyone you have met on a dating site, no matter what story they tell you.

- If you are suspicious of someone you have established contact with, use a Ghost Profile to check them out.
- Always arrange to meet first dates in well-lit public places, and remain in well-lit public areas throughout the whole of your time together.
- Don't make romantic commitments early, date the whole of your favourites list in consultation with your Buddy before you arrange a second date with anyone. If you think you're worth it, and you should think so, let them chase you.
- Interview each date for the demanding job of Life Partner. Their rewards will be great so make sure you only take the very best applicant.

Quitting Together

T his is where your adventure on the dating site comes to its end. It's been a fruitful and fun voyage, and now it's time to quit.

No partner will allow you, or want you to continue to chat to single strangers while you are with them, and assuming you have now found your life partner, the time has come to resign from the site.

Assuming you wouldn't want *your* new partner to continue hitting on strangers either, it makes sense if you quit together. This is the best way to do it. Get together in one of your homes, log on to the site one at a time, inform all your favourites and of course your Buddy's that you have been successful; wish them all good luck for the future, and say good-bye. Then cancel your memberships with the site. This way you both know that you have both quit, and neither of you will be going back.

If you don't do it this way, if you just quit at home, and then *tell* your new partner you have resigned, there may always be the suspicion that one of you is still on there. This happens, and the worst thing you can do now, after finding someone to love, is to allow suspicion to ruin what could be the best thing that has ever happened to you. Play fair, and resign together.

It is always hard saying goodbye, it's like leaving a job where you have been happy for a long time, where you have made great friends and had a lot of laughs along the way; it can be a tearful wrench; but it's the only way to prove to both yourself and to your new partner that the commitment you have made to each other is a serious and solid one.

Many people stay in touch with their ex-Buddy's after they find a partner and resign from the site. Your responsibility as an Online Buddy ends when you leave, but you may be asked to continue as an Offline Buddy. If this happens to you, this will be your choice of course, discuss the responsibility with your new partner before you agree to this, they may not be happy with you keeping in touch with old favourites from the dating site. Always remember your partner's wishes have to come before those of your favourites, including the wishes of your ex-Buddy.

Once you have quit the dating site together, you can start to begin a new life with a new partner in the real world, which was your original objective in selecting this book...So, you have been successful, well done, and good luck to the both of you!

Martin Slevin.

6. TYPES OF USERS

Whilst it is never wise to generalise about people, there are recognisable types of users, defined by their actions, who inhabit dating sites. Learning to spot the types will assist you in making decisions on how you deal with them.

The Buddy

Someone you like, who likes you, a clear favourite. Someone who started out as a potential partner, but has become a platonic friend. A person you can trust with your future safety, security and well-being. Accepting a Buddy incurs a mutual responsibility.

The Player

A person who has become stuck on the dating site out of habit. They have forgotten why they joined in the first place, and will probably never leave. They will chat with everyone, but are not really serious about finding a life partner as this will cause them to lose their source of amusement and entertainment. A favourite who will always have time to chat with you, but who continually makes excuses to avoid meeting you face to face, is probably a player. Give them a couple of chances, after that, dump them and move on.

The Predator

The serial dater. This is someone who is on there for fun, and fun only. They have no intention of finding a life partner as they can simply go from date to date without ever making a romantic commitment to anyone. The typical Predator collects girlfriends/ boyfriends like some people collect coins or stamps. Once it becomes apparent that they have "won" you, they will drop you like a hot potato. Predator's are the most difficult type to recognise, and your Buddy can help and advise you here. Typically the Predator will be very romantic and attractive when you first meet them, but once an emotional attachment starts to unfold, they will become increasingly more distant. It is at this point you can spot them.

The Pest

Someone who generally makes a nuisance of themselves. They tend to contact lots of people and will not leave you alone once contact has been established. This type finds it difficult to establish relationships generally, and will probably have a large amount of emotional baggage behind them. Use your Buddy to warn them off if they won't take no for an answer.

The Nutcase

E very dating site on the internet has a few of these. They are generally very easy to spot. They have huge emotional hang-ups, and past life baggage which will show early on. There is usually something "odd" in their profile, and they will make bizarre comments to you. Block them early, and report them to the site if they persist, or they become aggressive or offensive.

The Collector

S imilar to a Player but without the desire to break
your heart. The Collector simply gathers favourites
around them, and then never does anything with
them. The Collector tends to be a charming individual
and means no harm, but they will waste your time.
Friendly to chat to, but it's never going anywhere. You
can spot a Collector if you are in an instant messaging
conversation with them and it seems to take them a long
time to reply to each of your responses. It takes them
time to reply to you because they are holding numerous
conversations with their favourites at the same time as
chatting with you, and it is taking time to answer each
one in order. Dump this one early, they will waste both
your time and money.

The Bouncer

Like a rubber ball this one bounces from relationship to relationship. They were in love with the person before you, they will be in love with you, and they will fall in love with the one after you. The Bouncer loves being in love, but can't handle it in the real world. You can spot this one if you read between the lines of their conversations.

Always ask people you chat to how long they have been on the site, and if they have met anyone they really connected with yet.

The Rude and The Crude

Self explanatory. Offensive and inappropriate questions and remarks from the start. Block straight away, and report. Don't get into arguments, it's not worth it, it's a waste of your time and money.

The One

This is the prize, the one you came to find. How will you spot them when you make contact? Who knows? Persevere and offer respect to everyone you meet, keep your dignity at all times, and be honest, and maybe they'll spot you!

7. USEFUL PHRASES

Quite often people get stuck for something to say at an awkward moment, then the moment passes, and later on they think of the right response, only then it's too late. Here are a few tried and tested rejoinders you might like to try. You can reshape them to suit yourself, or use them exactly as they are, as you see fit at the time. Some of these have been suggested elsewhere in the book, and some are new; they are gathered here for ease of reference.

Recruiting A Buddy

"We've been chatting for some time now, and I really like you. I was wondering if you have ever heard of the Buddy Safety System for dating sites?"

If they respond, *"No"* then explain the mutual responsibilities of it to them. Ask them not to accept unless they will take it seriously, and in turn so will you. If they respond with, "*Yes*", then…

"*That's great! I have come to trust your judgement, and I would like to ask you to become my Buddy on here, what do you say?*"

When you Ask Them First

(Instant Messaging)

"*Hi. I hope I am not disturbing you by contacting you out of the blue like this, but I have read your profile, and really like the things you say about yourself, and I would welcome a chat with you, if you're not too busy right now. If you are, that's fine, I will understand perfectly.*"

Or

"*Hello. Do you have time for a chat right now? I will understand if it's inconvenient at the moment, but if you could suggest another time perhaps? I really like your profile and would love to chat with you for a while.*"

Or

"*Hey I really like your big nose!*" (Guaranteed a response) then…

"*I was only checking to make sure you had a great sense of humour before I let you talk to me…*"

Asking For Their Telephone Number

"We seem to be getting on well together, don't we? I would like to hear your voice and speak to you. Would it be OK for me to call you?"

If they seem unsure, or hesitant, or decline...

"OK, no problem, we can forget that idea then, so where were we...?"

If they agree and give you the number...

"That's great, I'm looking forward to speaking with you, shall I call right now?"

Speaking To Them On The Telephone For The First Time

"Hi, it's me! It's so interesting to have a voice to go with the face and the messages, don't you think?"

If you want to allow the relationship to develop after hearing their voice...

"It's been great chatting with you, I have to go now but it will be so much nicer whispering to you next time, now that we have talked like this. Let's chat again soon, bye bye."

If you do *not want* the relationship to develop after speaking to them...

"I have enjoyed speaking with you. But I have to go now, bye bye."

Asking Out A Favourite

"….We've been chatting for a good while now, and I would really like to meet you, what do you think?"

Or

"We seem to get on really well, how do you feel about taking things to the next level? I mean meeting for real?"

(E-Mailing)

"Hello. I came across your profile a few minutes ago, and just had to sit down and write to you! I really like what you have to say about yourself, and especially about the (naked mud wrestling) That sounds so interesting. I like your pictures too, the one (in the sweater) in particular. You look so relaxed. I will be on the site tomorrow night around nine, if you're around then perhaps we could have a chat?"

Or

"Hello. I have just read your profile, and noticed you like (horse riding)

I have always had a passion for (horse riding), and would love to chat with you about it when you have the time. If you would like to contact me, please do, we fellow (horse riders) should stick together!

When They Ask You First

(Accepting)

"Yes, Thank you. I would really like that."
Or
"I was wondering how long it would take you to ask me!"

(Postponing)

"I would like to chat with you, but I am really busy at the moment. I am sorry. Would you contact me again next time, and I will make sure I have the time for a chat, is that OK?"

Or

"I would like to chat with you, but I am really busy at the moment, can you give me (five/ten/fifteen) minutes and I will contact you back? Thanks for being so understanding. We'll have a chat in a little while."

(Declining)

"I am sorry. But you don't fit the type of person I am looking for on here. However, you do have a nice profile, and I wish you all the best of luck!"

(Explaining Your Decision To Decline)

"I am involved with someone on here at the moment, and am not accepting any new contacts for the time being. I hope you understand."

Dealing With A Pest

"I'm sorry but I am too busy to chat with you right now. I do have a number of people on here that I plan to spend some time with tonight, and I can't fit you in. Please don't contact me every time I am on here, if I have the time I will contact you next time, ok? Thanks for being in touch."

Then...

"I have told you I am not interested. Please do not continue to contact me. You are wasting both our times"

Then...

"I have now told you three times. I will not respond to you again. Should you continue to harass me like this I will contact the site and make a formal complaint about you. Good bye."

Informing The Date You Have A Buddy

"That was my Buddy from our dating site, he's just checking up to make sure I am ok. I told him I was meeting you here tonight, and he's checked out your profile. I hope you don't mind. Let's face it you can't be too careful these days, you could be a homicidal maniac for all I know!" (big smile!).

Challenging Uncomfortable Exchanges

"I really like talking to you, and I do want to get to know you better, but I am a little uncomfortable with the way this conversation is going right now. I am not really ready for this, and I would prefer it if we talked about something else for now. Is that OK?"

Applying The Brakes

"I can't believe we have come so far so soon, this is not really like me, and I feel a little out of control right now. Do you feel the same? I haven't changed my mind at all about developing this with you, and seeing where it goes, I just want to take it forward at a slower pace, is that ok?"

Saying Farewell To Your Buddy

(Tell them on the telephone)

"I wanted you to be the first to know that (new partner's name) and I have decided to make a commitment to each other, and we're resigning from the site together tonight. I wanted you to know that I deeply appreciate all your help, support, and encouragement and I will never forget you. Stay in touch if you want to, and let me know how you are getting on, I wish you the very best of luck."

Saying Farewell To Your Favourites

(Use onsite IM system)

"I just wanted to tell you that I have now found someone special, and I have made a commitment to them, so this is the last time I shall be on here. I wanted to thank you for being such a great friend during my time on this site, I will not forget you, but I have to play fair with my new partner, and we are resigning our memberships together tonight. Thanks once again for everything, and I wish you the very best of luck."

8. RECOMMENDED SITES

This is a list of sites either myself, or people I have spoken to have held memberships with and can recommend. The list is by no means complete or comprehensive, and I would urge you to search out sites for yourself; try as many as you like before selecting the one you feel most "at home" with. Remember you can join as many as you like for free, on a trial membership basis, before you have to pay any money, and so it is worth shopping around!

(In Alphabetical Order)

- asiafriendfinder.com

(For Asian and Oriental seekers, also those looking for an Asian or Oriental partner)

- datingforparents.com

(Single Parents dating site)

- loopylove.com
- match.com
- meetic.co.uk
- msn.match.com
- trustcupid.com
- Udate.com

About the Author

Martin Slevin has spend two years interviewing hundreds of people on dating sites around the world. After his own twelve year marriage came to an end he joined a dating site to see what all the fuss was about.

After a year he met his new partner, and has now started to build a new life, but not before going through the many ups and downs of internet dating.

Martin has written this book so that its readers can avoid the pitfalls most people fall into, and also so they can take short cuts; they won't have to do everything by trial and error, which can be a painful learning process, they can simply do things the right way, the first time.

"I wish a book like this had been around when I first started Internet Dating, it would have made the whole process so much easier, less fraught and more efficient" Said Martin.